THE TESTIMONY OF JESUS:

THE SPIRIT OF PROPHECY

Book 1

as spoken to one of His servant scribes

THE TESTIMONY OF JESUS:
THE SPIRIT OF PROPHECY-Book 1
[Revelation 19:10]
as spoken to one of
His servant scribes

Scribed by Laverne C. Ihm

Gold Spirit Ministries, Inc.
2627 N. 114th Street
Milwaukee, WI 53226

Published by Gold Spirit Ministries, Inc. in conjunction with
Ransom Publishing House, Inc.
A subsidiary of Kingdom of Heaven Christian Ministries, Inc.
Milwaukee, Wisconsin, U.S.A.
Printed in U.S.A.

Ransom Publishing House, Inc. is a Christian publisher dedicated to take the Kingdom message to the local church and beyond. We have a vision for Kingdom truth and Kingdom principles to be provided to church leaders that will help them evangelize, disciple and mature the saints according to Ephesians 4:11-13: "And he gave some, apostles; and some, prophets; and some, evangelists; and some, pastors and teachers; For the perfecting of the saints, for the work of the ministry, for the edifying of the body of Christ: Till we all come in the unity of the faith, and of the knowledge of the Son of God, unto a perfect man, unto the measure of the stature of the fulness of Christ."

Library of Congress Cataloging-in-Publication Data
Ihm, Laverne C., scribe
THE TESTIMONY OF JESUS: THE SPIRIT OF PROPHECY - Book 1
as spoken to one of His servant scribes
ISBN 0-9672637-0-0

Distributed by Gold Spirit Ministries, Inc., 2627 N. 114th Street, Milwaukee,
WI 53226

Book Layout and Production Coordinated By
Write Hand Publishing · www.writehand.com

About the Cover

After seeking the Lord, the idea for this cover came very easily. It was not by my might, but it was by the Lord's Spirit that I received the inspiration. It was gratifying that God spoke to me through several people. And this is precisely how the Lord has worked through the life of Laverne "Vern" Ihm. The Spirit of Prophecy is the testimony of Jesus. In the Lord we live and move and have our being and this is how we are a testimony to others. I believe the cover clearly illustrates the brilliant, illuminating power of the Holy Spirit as God works through the lives of His children. The dove is a symbol of God's healing power. Malachi 4:2 says, *"But for you who revere my name, the sun of righteousness will rise with healing in its wings . . ."* The Lord reveals His glory through His saints as we allow the Holy Spirit to have His way in our lives. This surrender is what I was pleased to have captured on the cover. Psalm 68:13 says, *". . . the wings of my dove are sheathed with silver, its feathers with shining gold."* It is evident that the Lord deserves the glory for this book, its cover, and all that He has done through Vern. I am blessed and honored to have been asked to do this cover and I thank the Lord for His divine touch.

Tony M. Meister, Artist

CONTENTS

Dedication and Appreciation

I dedicate this book, the first of a series, to the King of kings and the Lord of lords, and for His glory to be manifested in His saints until His Kingdom is firmly established upon this earth as it is in heaven. To HIM be all the glory forever and ever! Amen! Rev. 12:11 says: "They [the saints] overcame him [the devil] by the blood of the Lamb and by the word of their testimony."[1]

My last name is: **Ihm**, which in German means: **To Him**. My grandfather often said: "Von **Ihm** kam ich. Zu **Ihm** werde ich wiedergehen." In English this means: "**From Him** I came. **To Him** I shall return again." This is reflective of Rom. 11:36: "For **from him** and through him and **to him** are all things." **To Him** be the glory forever! Amen. Only when "**ihm**" is at the beginning of a sentence or when it refers to God is it capitalized! Hence, my capitalized name and my life says: **TO HIM** BE ALL THE GLORY FOREVER! This book and my life are dedicated **TO HIM**!

Yes, both this book and I are dedicated to His Divine Majesty and His Royal Kingdom People whom He has taught to communicate with Him continually, singing "psalms, hymns and spiritual songs."[2] I appreciate and thank those faithful prayer partners who had spiritual vision enough to stand so loyally and courageously with me fixing "our eyes on Jesus"[3] during the blackest of

---

[1]Testimony according to *Webster's* means a solemn declaration or affirmation made to establish some fact; affirmation; declaration; evidence, especially validating evidence; attestation; act of testifying; open attestation; profession.
[2] Eph. 5:19

storms and the brightest of dawns. All of my faithful prayer partners shall remain anonymous in this book, and therefore to protect that anonymity, wherever a name appears, I have given them fictitious names. These people will recognize who they are and will want no glory on this earth for themselves. Their reward shall be apportioned to them as "a treasure in heaven that will not be exhausted, where no thief comes near and no moth destroys." [4]

Public personages, however, are identified as themselves. And I am very grateful to each of those who have ministered to me, mentored me, prayed for and with me, worshiped with me, pastored me and have sown into my life. Of special acknowledgement is my wife, Jean, my daughter, Carla, and my parents, Frank and Bernice Ihm, both of whom have gone to their eternal reward and are among the "great cloud of witnesses" surrounding us. Their reaping shall be great, for they will reap what they have sown. Just as the natural seed of the botanical kingdom is multiplied, so, too, is there multiplication when you enter into the supernatural spiritual realm, as St. Paul says in Gal. 6:7,8: "Do not be deceived: God is not mocked. A man reaps what he sows. The one who sows to please his sinful nature, from that nature will reap destruction; the one who sows to please the Spirit, from the Spirit will reap eternal life."

Also I thank in advance any of you readers who will join us in prayer wherever you are, seeking His perfect will for us and yourselves: "Sing and make music in your

[3] Heb. 12:2
[4] Lk. 12:33

heart to the Lord, always giving thanks to God the Father for everything, in the name of our Lord Jesus Christ." [5] Join us in prayer for the "anointing to spoil" the enemy [6] and to "subdue nations" [7] for His Glory by preaching the gospel of the kingdom that Jesus preached. "Thy kingdom come; Thy will be done on earth, as it is in heaven." [8] [KJV]

Lastly, but not least, I thank those who proof-read, corrected errors and made critical contributions to the flow of the text. I mention particularly, Jean, my wife, Carla, my daughter, Tony Meister, my friend and artist who did the masterful cover for this book, Elder Dick Gibbons, a fellow elder, Pastor James Paden, my beloved friend and dear pastor, and the Holy Spirit, my beloved teacher who guided me with inspiration, counsel and wisdom.

His Servant Scribe,[9] Laverne C. Ihm
In The Year of Our Lord, 1999

---

[5] Eph. 5:19-20
[6] Ex. 3:21-22; 12:36
[7] Heb. 11:33
[8] Mt. 6:10
[9] A scribe is defined by *Webster's* as an official or public writer acting usually as a clerk; a copier of manuscripts; a penman; author; writer; journalist.

FORWARD

Laverne Ihm is truly the epitome of the greatest in the kingdom being the servant of all. In this first installment of a series of books, he gives a riveting testimony that great faith and great victories come out of great tests and trials.

Thomas Jefferson once stated that "he that knows nothing is nearer to the truth than he whose mind is filled with falsehood and errors." "The Testimony of Jesus" is the real life-story of a man whose heart was to serve God from his youth but had to overcome the ignorance and deception of religious tradition to do so.

The Holy Bible says "the testimony of Jesus is the spirit of prophecy." (Rev.19:10) This book was conceived through the words of many prophets that I was personally present to hear speak prophetic seeds into the spiritual womb of the author. I believe the voice of King Jesus will be heard through one of His loyal scribes speaking truth to His loyal subjects in the body of Christ and those who will be heirs of salvation. The reader will not just be reading another man's story but will see a demonstration of God's glory.

I highly recommend this book as a resource for the seeker of truth and those that hunger and thirst for righteousness. I know the author and I am an eyewitness of the work the Lord has wrought in his life. I am also privileged to serve as his pastor.

Pastor James W. Paden
Kingdom of Heaven Christian Ministries
Milwaukee, Wisconsin

14

THE TESTIMONY OF JESUS: THE SPIRIT OF PROPHECY [10] as spoken to one of His servant scribes- Book 1

INTRODUCTION

The Lord is looking for a few humble men; He will not share the Glory that belongs to Him with any man. Yet the Lord wants His Glory known to men. He wants to prepare His people for things to come in the end times. "I am the Lord, that is my name! I will not give my Glory to another or my praise to idols. See, the former things have taken place, and new things I declare; before they spring into being I announce them to you."[11]

One of the dangers of writing a personal testimony is some will mistakenly want to praise the creature instead of the Creator. The purpose of this testimony is to glorify and praise God for what HE IS DOING THROUGH HIS HUMBLE SERVANT. My model and master is Christ Jesus, who "humbled himself."[12] My prayer to each person who reads this book [hereafter referred to as *The Testimony of Jesus – Book 1*] is that "every

---

[10] Prophecy according to *Webster's* is speaking for another, especially for God; like a seer; being an effective spokesman for a group or a cause; [in Jewish & Christian Theology]: being inspired by God to speak in his name. Prophecy means the work or vocation of a prophet; utterance of a prophet; a declaration of something to come; prediction. It is one of the gifts of the Holy Spirit which will be discussed later.

[11] Is. 42:8

[12] Phil. 2:8

tongue confess that Jesus Christ is Lord, to the glory of God the Father."[13]

In 1987, God plainly drew my attention to my divine destiny of having an "anointing to spoil" the enemy. This calling was clearly depicted in the Bible when the Israelites overcame and destroyed their enemies as Moses led them out of Egypt, thus spoiling the Egyptians.

All Christians are called to have that anointing to spoil the enemy, who is the devil. Some people have the anointing to spoil the enemy through intercession, some through praise, some through dance and music, some in evangelism, or in transferring the wealth from the wicked to the righteous to preach the gospel to all nations, among others. We all are called to spoil the devil in whatever calling God has given us so we can glorify the Lord, manifest His Glory and establish His kingdom on earth as it is in heaven.

One thing I did not realize at that time, however, was that God was calling me to walk by faith, not by sight, on a road of the miraculous to manifest His Glory in His calling.

What the reader will see in *The Testimony Of Jesus - Book I* is out of the ordinary; and it is beyond human comprehension. It is the Divine Master at work! But know, dear reader, my beloved Lord is for all "the

---

[13] Phil. 2:11

same yesterday and today and forever."[14] You, too, are called by Him to manifest His Glory as He wills in your life. Surrender to Him, walk in the Spirit and open your eyes to His miracles in your life. We all have a divine destiny.

This is not an autobiography, but a testimony of Jesus. A testimony of Jesus refers to the life of one who walks Jesus' steps in a similar fashion, paying the price of the cross. It is a prophetic spiritual journey of Him walking forth today through one of His servants who listens and obeys. This journey documents through the eyes of faith what is really happening in the spiritual realm while we await events to unfold that will be revealed and perceived in the physical realm by both the natural and the spiritual eye.

Those that believe Jesus still lives and works in us will be blessed. Skeptics will leave in bewilderment. But Jesus promised "the one who has faith in me . . . will do even greater things than these,"[15] and He "chose the foolish things of the world to shame the wise; God chose the weak things of the world to shame the strong. He chose the lowly things of this world and the despised things—to nullify the things that are, so that no one may boast before him."[16] And I am one of the foolish, lowly and despised things of this world.

Rom. 1:17 says, "The just will live by faith." The

---

[14] Heb. 13:8

[15] Jn. 4:12

[16] 1 Cor. 1:27

unsaved cannot fathom this because the carnal mind cannot comprehend spiritual truths. A spiritual mind, one of righteousness, is needed as Rom. 1:17 clearly states, "For in the gospel a righteousness from God is revealed, a righteousness that is by faith from first to last, just as it is written: 'The righteous will live by faith.'" And 1 Cor. 2:4,5 says, "My message and my preaching were not with wise and persuasive words, but with a demonstration of the Spirit's power, so that your faith might not rest on men's wisdom, but on God's power."

One way God has revealed His miraculous power to me has been through journaling. Journaling is simply recording God's word as it is spoken to one who sits in His presence, listens to what the Spirit of God is saying today, and writes it down.

Journaling consists merely of being in the presence of God, and His thoughts become your thoughts. Just as Jesus received and knew the thoughts and the will of the Father, and therefore did only what He saw the Father doing, so, too, while journaling we can know the mind and the heart of our Father and do what we see the Father doing. Jesus and the Father did not have to speak verbally to each other because they thought the same thoughts. Jesus said: "I and the Father are one."[17] Also: "[The Son] can only do what he sees his Father doing."[18]

---

[17] Jn. 10:30

[18] Jn. 5:19

Journaling God's word should never be contrary to His Biblical truth found in the Scriptures, for God never contradicts Himself; since He is the author of all truth, He can never tell a lie. For years I struggled with the attempt of flowing freely at journaling, but the struggle ended, and the flow began, when a prophetic person told me: "Just take a pen and paper; put the date on the paper and expect God to speak. Don't try to analyze it while it flows; test and discern the word later." That broke the pent-up dam and now words just continue to flow freely from my spirit-man.[19]

In addition to journaling, God has revealed His sovereign purpose for my life through prophetic words spoken by many. Even as it pertained to writing this book, I have received numerous prophetic words that have supernaturally confirmed God's will for me to share this testimony at this time. I encourage you to read these prophecies in the EPILOGUE.

This book, *The Testimony of Jesus – Book 1*, most likely shall be a trilogy. Book 1, along with its appendices, deals with the background for the revelation of God's glory in my life until 1992; hopefully subsequent books will deal with the journaling and prophetic words spoken thereafter. And, the Lord willing, Book 2 and 3 [and other books as the Lord leads me] shall deal with the fulfillment and manifestation of the prophetic words spoken and written, whenever the

---

[19] Man is composed of body, soul and spirit; the spirit part is referred to as the spirit-man which was created by God to be in charge of the soul and body. (1 Thes. 5:23; Rom. 6:4-8))

Lord releases me to share those things.

Whenever "we" or "us" appears in this book, it refers to my wife and myself if not otherwise noted.

PREFACE

The excitement all began over twelve years ago, in February 1987. At that time I received my first prophetic word from an itinerant preacher, Jim Partington, who is from Wales, England. He travels the world, walking the land, preaching the gospel to many nations.[20] Though the prophecy was never recorded word for word, my wife and I immediately attempted to reconstruct the theme and concepts as soon as we left the meeting.[21] In summary, the essence of the prophetic message was:

Amen. Amen. Amen. For the Lord saith: I am preparing you for a new calling. When you were young, honors, awards and recognition were very important to you. But that phase of your life is past. Now the Lord is about to take you through a valley of hardship to purify you and to prepare your heart for His appointed time when He will lift you up to great heights and bless you abundantly. You are being called to dispense great wealth anonymously for His Kingdom. Amen.

Shortly thereafter, I began writing down my testimony and journaling, though not daily. But as time went on, I became thirsty for His word and soon jour-

---

[20] Jim Partington has published his autobiography, *Walking The Land*.

[21] Most prophetic words, when recorded on tape, have been preserved as spoken and not corrected for grammar, etc., in order to preserve the accuracy of the prophetic message and meaning. Those not recorded on tape are pieced together as best as those who heard it can recall.

naled almost daily. Only significant prophetic journal-ings, and only those prophecies that explain some of that prophetic journaling, appear in this book. Some others may appear in other books that the Lord will prompt me to write at a later date.

This book is not written just for Christian believ-ers, but for those that are not yet believers, including Jews, Muslims, Buddhists, Hindus, Shintos, spiritists, animists, agnostics and all other indigenous and reli-gious groups, for Jesus said: "*Man* does not live on bread alone, but on every word that comes from the mouth of the Lord."[22] He didn't say: *"Christians"* shall live by every word that proceeds from the mouth of God; He said *"Man!"* So every *man* will be held accountable to God for every word that proceeds forth from His mouth. The testimony of Jesus is for every man!

I see there are only two kinds of people on earth,[23] those who are believers and those who are about to become believers. Which one are you? You can easily become a believer by accepting Jesus as your Savior and Lord by confessing aloud:

Heavenly Father, forgive all my sins! Jesus, come into my heart and make me the kind of person You want me to be. Thank You for saving me today.[24]

---

[22] Mt. 4:4; Lk. 4:4

[23] This appears in the booklet by Charles and Frances Hunter entitled, *There Are Two Kinds Of...*, published by and available from Hunter Books, 201 McClellan Road, Kingwood, TX 77339-2710.

Then ask the Lord to lead you to the church in which He wants you to fellowship, worship and grow spiritually. He heard your sincere prayer. And just as easily, you can hear His voice[25] just as I hear Him with ease when I journal.

Whether you are a believer or not a believer, others including myself, are praying for you. For many obey the word of God which says,

I urge, then, first of all, that requests, prayers, intercession and thanksgiving be made for everyone—for kings and all those in authority, that we may live peaceful and quiet lives in all godliness and holiness. This is good, and pleases God our Savior, who wants all men to be saved and to come to a knowledge of the truth. For there is one God and one mediator between God and men, the man Christ Jesus, who gave himself as a ransom

---

[24] Romans 10:9-11: That if you confess with your mouth, "Jesus is Lord," and believe in your heart that God raised him from the dead, you will be saved. For it is with your heart that you believe and are justified, and it is with your mouth that you confess and are saved. As the Scripture says, "Anyone who trusts in him will never be put to shame."

Acts 2:38-39: Peter replied, "Repent and be baptized, every one of you, in the name of Jesus Christ for the forgiveness of your sins. And you will receive the gift of the Holy Spirit. 39 The promise is for you and your children and for all who are far off--for all whom the Lord our God will call."

[25] John 10:14-16,27,28: "I am the good shepherd; I know my sheep and my sheep know me--just as the Father knows me and I know the Father--and I lay down my life for the sheep. I have other sheep that are not of this sheep pen. I must bring them also. They too will listen to my voice, and there shall be one flock and one shepherd. My sheep listen to my voice; I know them, and they follow me. I give them eternal life, and they shall never perish; no one can snatch them out of my hand.

for all men—the testimony given in its proper time.[26]

The testimony of Jesus is for every man.

Please enjoy the words of the Master! He loves you with His infinite love, and He wants you to know Him even as He knows you! And He has much He wants to share with you; so spend time with Him! Set a priority on your time with Jesus over and above those things that so easily distract you and consume precious time that could be spent with Him. He loves your time spent with Him! He is waiting for you to come!

---

[26] 1 Tim. 2:1-6

CHAPTER 1

From the Beginning—A Background

My wife and I came out of the Roman Catholic tradition. Both of us were born into and raised in staunch Catholic families; my wife in the southeastern Ohio coal mining country, and I in the lead-zinc mining district of southwestern Wisconsin. As young people, we were both saved in the Catholic denomination and dedicated our lives to serving the Lord as we knew how. At the age of fourteen, each of us desiring to serve the Lord in ministry, left home to enter preparational training.

Even as a youngster in the third grade I had a great desire to serve the Lord. As a student in St. Clement's Catholic school in Lancaster, Wisconsin, my heart would burn with love for Jesus as Sister Aquiline or Father Felix A. Hoffman would teach us about God the Father and Jesus, His Son.

One day we had a retreat at school that focused on what God was calling each of us to do when we grew up into adulthood. I shared that I wanted to be a priest, because I thought that would be the best way I could show my great love for Jesus. From that day forward my focus of serving Jesus was firmly fixed.

At home my parents were godly people, kneeling down every night to pray together as a family. This made an indelible mark on my impressionable heart. I remember many times quietly sharing my love for Jesus and His mother Mary.

I had a great respect for Mary, Jesus' mother, but I never

felt I was worshipping her or giving her any undue homage or honor that Jesus Himself would not have given her. I felt that her mandate to the servants at the wedding feast of Cana was great advice: ***"Do whatever he tells you."*** [27] Would that everyone would heed her advice and do whatever Jesus says!

My respect for her was similar to that which I gave to my mother who bore 12 of us children. I never understood it when people sometimes accused me as a Catholic boy of worshipping Mary. I never did, though I believe some Catholics may have a very distorted view of Mary that even hurts the heart of Jesus Himself. But then I have come to find out as I grew up that every denomination has some doctrine that is false, man-made or from a tradition of man that is not from God.

In fact, if every one of us looked honestly at the Church of Jesus, the one true Church that He established, and compared it to any one present-day denomination, we would have little left if we threw out all man-made teachings and traditions. Even Jesus in His day chastised His spiritual leaders who were not only leading people astray with man-made doctrine and rules, but were keeping others from entering into the kingdom: ***"For I say unto you, That except your righteousness shall exceed [the righteousness] of the scribes and Pharisees, ye shall in no case enter into the kingdom of heaven."*** [28] Jesus said that! I didn't say it! Jesus did! He hates legalism, and we need to hate what God hates!

In the fall of 1947, I entered Salvatorian Seminary at St. Nazianz, Wisconsin, and subsequently graduated four years later. Salvatorian Seminary offered me a high school classical educa-

---

[27] Jn. 2:5

tion with a strong emphasis as a preparatory institution training students for the Roman Catholic priesthood. In the fall of 1951, I stayed home from school because I had a strong desire to get married some day. I was torn between mandatory celibacy required by the Catholic Church and marriage. With some encouragement from the parish priests I entered Holy Cross Seminary in LaCrosse, Wisconsin, for college and received a bachelor's degree [B.A.] in philosophy.

The Lord was working His plan in the lives of my wife and myself even then. That same Fall of '51, my wife at the age of fourteen came via the Baltimore & Ohio Railroad, traveling over 500 miles, to the Holy Family Convent in Manitowoc, Wisconsin. This is where Jean was to begin her high school preparatory training as a Catholic sister in the Order of St. Francis (OSF).

In 1955, I entered St. Francis Major Seminary in Milwaukee, Wisconsin, to complete four years of theology. That same year, my wife entered Silver Lake College in Manitowoc, Wisconsin, to begin her college education. Two years later, in 1957, she was placed into her teaching career as a grade school teacher, completing her college education in the ensuing summer school classes.

On May 30, 1959, I was ordained a Catholic priest for the Diocese of Madison, Wisconsin. I served as an associate priest to several parishes and chaplain of mental institutions in southwestern Wisconsin for nine years. I was subsequently appointed pastor of St. Thomas Church in Potosi, Wisconsin, and superintendent of the joint St. Andrew-Thomas Catholic school, positions I held for two years until my resignation in June of 1970.

---

[28] Mt. 5:20 [KJV]

It was here that I was awakened to the fact that there was more to Christianity than I had been experiencing. The Vatican II Council's documents had been introducing fresh, welcome, but radical, changes within the Catholic Church in an attempt to bring spiritual renewal and revival that was long overdue. But, the people were slow to accept them and oftentimes reluctant to change accordingly.

Many would not be moved out of their comfort zones. A strong mentality that "I know all I want to know about religion; leave me alone, and don't bother me with the truth" existed among many people. They did not want their comfort zones disturbed with new life. Vitality was not an option to the dead state of mediocrity, ignorance and the deception which so easily leads to a complacent lifestyle. People must realize that religion is not simply adhering to a set of ancient traditions, but it is living in a relationship with the Lord. It is more than going to church every Sunday, not killing anybody, being a "nice guy" or "nice gal." Once we realize that God is more concerned *about our relationship with Him* than He is *about what we can do for Him*, then we will walk in liberty.

The Bible in 2 Corinthians 3:17 says ***"where the Spirit of the Lord is, there is liberty."*** [KJV] In Galatians 5:13 it says, ***"You, my brothers, were called to be free. But do not use your freedom to indulge the sinful nature; rather, serve one another in love."*** The King James Version puts it this way: ***"For, brethren, you have been called unto liberty; only [use] not liberty for an occasion to the flesh, but by love serve one another."***

There was a spirit of religion influencing many of my

parishioners. This religious mindset is man's idea of religion and it leaves no opportunity for true spirituality or true liberty to serve God and others. This type of religion thinks if we are legalistic, we can be good and earn heaven without ever knowing the true God intimately. What a deceitful spirit! *"Pure religion and undefiled before God and the Father is this, To visit the fatherless and widows in their affliction, [and] to keep himself unspotted from the world."* [29] [KJV]

So I say, live by the Spirit, and you will not gratify the desires of the sinful nature. For the sinful nature desires what is contrary to the Spirit, and the Spirit what is contrary to the sinful nature. They are in conflict with each other, so that you do not do what you want. But if you are led by the Spirit, you are not under law. [30]

The spirit of religion and the spirit of tradition can keep people in a small cage like the little bird described in a book written by John Osteen, entitled *"How To Flow in the Super Supernatural."* Osteen tells of a little bird that was hatched in a cage, and never knew there was anything more to life than his confinement. But one day when he noticed he had wings, he knew he was created to fly. But all he could do was eat his bird seed and swing on his swing. One day when the cage door was open, he flew out and through a window, and he knew he was set free to do what he was created to do—fly!

Many of us are hatched in our denominational bird cage; we sit in our denominational cage, and we swing on our denomi-

---

[29] Jas. 1:27
[30] Gal. 5:16-18

national swing, and eat our denominational bird seed. But God is putting such a hunger for truth in the hearts of His people that many are flying out of their cages and seeking a wider experience for that which they have been created—to fly high as eagles. We are sons of God—and heirs of the King.

If I only had known then what I know now, I might have been able to provide the true seed of the word to the people, and deliver them of that religious spirit and set them free!

I am not advocating anyone to leave the Church; just get set free! If your local church is a dead dumb church, please fly out the window and seek the Lord for the place where you can be fed more than denominational bird seed.[31]

In the late '60s, even though a priest, not only did I not understand deliverance from spirits that keep people prisoners in their cage, but I still had not yet come to an understanding of how to do *effective* intercessory spiritual warfare prayer.[32] Therefore, I became very frustrated with pastoring a group of people who were strongly influenced by a few pro-active ultra-conservatives who were controlled by religious spirits and had **"a form of godliness, but denied the power thereof."** [33]

I felt like Jesus did when He confronted the scribes and Pharisees:

But woe unto you, scribes and Pharisees, hyp-

---

[31] For more on this subject, please read the two chapters on freedom in the Spirit, entitled, *Super Gifts Freely Given and The Fruit of The Holy Spirit.*

[32] See Chapter 5 for an in-depth explanation of spiritual warfare prayer.

[33] 2 Tim. 3:5

ocrites! for ye shut up the kingdom of heaven against men: for ye neither go in [yourselves], neither suffer ye them that are entering to go in. Woe unto you, scribes and Pharisees, hypocrites! for ye devour widows' houses, and for a pretence make long prayer: therefore ye shall receive the greater damnation. Woe unto you, scribes and Pharisees, hypocrites! for ye compass sea and land to make one proselyte, and when he is made, ye make him twofold more the child of hell than yourselves . . . [Ye] blind guides, which strain at a gnat, and swallow a camel.[34] [KJV]

Paul described people with a similar spirit that he met in his day:

They profess that they know God; but in works they deny [him], being abominable, and disobedient, and unto every good work reprobate.[35] [KJV]

It was also there in Potosi that I met Sister Jean Reischman, OSF, who later became my wife. After teaching in Wisconsin, Ohio and West Virginia, Sister Jean was serving as school principal, teacher and Superior to the Sisters residing and teaching at Potosi. She, too, had experienced similar frustration and was planning to leave the religious order in June 1970, though unbeknownst to anyone.

In December, 1969, I wrote to my bishop asking for an indefinite leave of absence from the active ministry, telling him I

---

34 Mt. 23:13-15, 24
35 Tit. 1:16 [KJV]

was returning to the University of Wisconsin-Milwaukee for a Master's degree [M. A.] in rehabilitation counseling with an emphasis on alcoholism treatment. I left on June 1st with no regrets and no ill feelings toward anyone.

In March, 1970, Sister Jean brought a document from the Vatican in Rome dispensing her from her vows and allowing her to go into secular status. She brought that to me as her pastor for my signature. I was shocked and surprised. During the Easter recess she then went to Ohio for several interviews seeking a teaching position. But nothing opened up and she returned not knowing what to do after June 1st. I told her of my plans to go to Milwaukee for schooling and I felt confident that I could count on many of my former seminary classmates who served as associate priests in Milwaukee to assist her in getting a teaching position in a Catholic school. She came to Milwaukee in June and much to the surprise of both of us, I was a "persona non grata" in the eyes of several of my former classmates. We were looked upon with great suspicion by many and treated by some as traitors for leaving the active ministry. Needless to say, no position opened up in the parochial schools.

So Jean went to several public school districts and by that August had received two contract offers that were very good teaching opportunities. She chose a Milwaukee suburban district, where she taught for 29 years.[36] Jean and I began to date that summer of 1970, and later we chose to marry on February 27, 1971, with Father Jerry Memmel officiating.

After finishing the Master's program at UW-Milwaukee with my M. A. degree, I was asked to head up two new departments at DePaul Rehabilitation Hospital, a position which I held for five years. Following that, I initiated my career as a registered representative [commonly known as a stockbroker of securities] and as an insurance agent.

It was only after we left the active ministry that we were baptized in the Holy Spirit in the Catholic tradition. And then the Lord really began doing a work in us.

Though I had loved the Lord dearly over the many years in the seminary and in the active ministry as a priest, and had an intimate relationship with Him, I did not have a love for His word. And this lack of a loving, working knowledge of the living word found in the Scriptures kept me from maturing into the deep, deep relationship with the Lord which I later found.

I encourage every one to read the Bible and meditate on the word of God every day for at least 15 minutes. We cannot go without physical food for a whole week. Why starve spiritually when the Bible is so available daily to feed us spiritually? It is food for the hungry spirit-man, and the Lord really speaks to us through His word. At times the print seems to become larger or even brighter, and I know this is a 'rhema' word, a word spoken to me personally from God. Sometimes it seems as though I never had read that passage before because it took on such a relevant meaning that day! That's the Lord speaking through His rhema, or current word, to my situation! Awesome! God is awesome!

It was not long after God spoke to us through His word that He began to speak to us through other people as well.

Both Jean and I had received a prophetic word that we as a cou-

---

36 After 42 years, Jean retired from teaching full-time in June, 1999, having taught in Catholic schools for 13 years and 29 years in the Wauwatosa Public School District, teaching all 8 grades during those years.

ple would be used mightily by God to minister to many Catholic people.[37] This led us to believe that we had to stay within the Catholic denominational tradition to fulfill our destiny. So for many years we would faithfully attend Mass at St. Joseph's Catholic Church in Wauwatosa on Saturday evenings and we would go elsewhere on Sunday to other Spirit-filled churches that could feed us solid meat[38] in the word.

Finally, we came to the conclusion that when the Lord did tell us to leave, we did not have to leave the Church Jesus established; we were just leaving a denomination. We came to understand that His Church is not any one denomination, nor any one organization, but an organism that is led by the Holy Spirit through the five-fold ministries Jesus established.[39] His Church is the Body of Christ comprised not of denominations or divisions, but of believing Christians who are willing to come out of their comfort zones into the unity Jesus prayed for[40] and learn of His word and His calling on each of our lives to preach the gospel to the utter ends

---

[37] Over the last ten years we had received several messages about ministering specifically to Catholic people through persons speaking prophetically, the most notable and clear words came on November 18, 1993 and on December 17, 1998 through Owen Johnson. See **EPILOGUE** in the back of the book.

[38] 1 Cor. 3:1-4: And I, brethren, could not speak unto you as unto spiritual, but as unto carnal, [even] as unto babes in Christ. 2 I have fed you with milk, and not with meat: for hitherto ye were not able [to bear it], neither yet now are ye able. 3 For ye are yet carnal: for whereas [there is] among you envying, and-strife, and divisions, are ye not carnal, and walk as men? 4 For while one saith, I am of Paul; and another, I [am] of Apollos; are ye not carnal? [KJV]

[39] Eph. 4:11-13: It was he who gave some to be **apostles**, some to be **prophets**, some to be **evangelists,** and some to be **pastors** and **teachers**, 12 to prepare God's people for works of service, so that the body of Christ may be built up 13 **until we all reach unity** in the faith and in the knowledge of the Son of God **and become mature**, attaining to the whole measure of the fullness of Christ.

[40] At the Last Supper Jesus after Jesus taught: "I am the true vine, and my Father is the gardener. He cuts off every branch in me that bears no fruit, while every

34

of the earth! We are the Church! We are the Bride of Christ! And He wants a mature Bride!

His Church is not hierarchical but relational! We are the Body of Christ! We believe that there is one true universal Church, made up of genuine believers, but this one universal Church is also composed of many local Churches in given localities. These Churches are under the sovereign headship of the Lord Jesus Christ, exercising autonomous government under Him, administering all its local affairs and ministry, as well as the propagation of the Gospel.[41]

In answer to our friends and relatives who ask us, "Why did you leave the Church?" we respond, "We never left the Church! We left a denomination!" We were hungry and we wanted to be fed rich spiritual food.

Although there are believers in every denomination, not everyone in every denomination have made Jesus the Lord of their lives, nor are all well fed believers! There is more to salvation than just going to church, or thinking that you are a "good person!" You no more become a saved Christian when you walk into a Christian church than you become a car when you step into a garage! We need to find out the requirements of Jesus for salvation! See **Appendix A: Articles of Faith** in the back of this book.

---

branch that does bear fruit he prunes so that it will be even more fruitful. You are already clean because of the word I have spoken to you. Remain in me, and I will remain in you. No branch can bear fruit by itself; it must remain in the vine. Neither can you bear fruit unless you remain in me," Jesus prayed for unity of His disciples in Jn. 17: 11: I will remain in the world no longer, but they are still in the world, and I am coming to you. Holy Father, protect them by the power of your name--the name you gave me--so **that they may be one** as we are one. [Emphasis mine]

[41] Acts 15:22; with Matthew 16:18; 18:15-20

Friend, do you have a personal relationship with Jesus? If not, you can be assured of your salvation by accepting Jesus as both your Savior and as your Lord by professing it with your mouth and believeing it in your heart![42] If you have not professed aloud the footnote below, please do so now! The rest of this book will open your eyes to many truths, which may be new to you. And they will bless you.

When the Lord led us from the Catholic denomination, the Lord spoke clear instructions to me. On the Saturday evening of April 25, 1992, the Lord told me our family was to go to Brookfield Assembly of God for worship in the morning. So beginning Sunday, April 26, 1992, we faithfully attended that church at the direction of the Lord.

I wrote a letter to the pastor of St. Joseph's Catholic Church explaining our decision of discontinuing our membership there in obedience to the word of God. Brookfield Assembly of God became our church until January 31, 1995, when the Lord told us to leave there. At that point we had no idea where we were to worship after that. So the next Sunday, February 5th, my wife, my daughter and I worshipped and sought the Lord for direction in our living room. What happened next was the formation of a church by the Lord Himself and it was truly awesome. Details of that wonderful experience will be treated in a later book, the Lord willing.

---

[42] Rom. 9:9-11: That if you confess with your mouth, "Jesus is Lord," and believe in your heart that God raised him from the dead, you will be saved. 10 For it is with your heart that you believe and are justified, and it is with your mouth that you confess and are saved. 11 As the Scripture says, "Anyone who trusts in him will never be put to shame." Profess this aloud and be saved: **"Heavenly Father, forgive all my sins! Jesus, My Risen Savior, come into my heart and make me the kind of person You want me to be. Thank You for saving me today. I accept your saving grace and I recognize You as my Lord!"**

What we did not realize all the while we were in the Catholic tradition was the powerful influence the spirit of religion and the spirit of tradition had over our lives, keeping us from being set free in the Holy Spirit! Saints, it is great to be set free of every spirit that hinders us from advancing in the Kingdom of God! But if your denomination doesn't recognize influence of spirits over people, even Christian people, or doesn't practice deliverance or operate in the gifts of the Holy Spirit, in essence that denomination does not believe it. Therefore, denomination-alism is believing and teaching only part of God's word, which in practice is keeping those saints as immature babes!

I'm speaking from experience, and I am not trying to judge anyone! Jesus said, *"Do not judge, and you will not be judged."*[43] James tells us, *"Mercy triumphs over judgment!"*[44] We all need God's mercy and deliverance because we all are sinners.

I experienced a heavy spirit of religion over me and did not know it was there! I believe that the spirit of religion is present in every denominational church group that denies the whole truth of the Gospel by denying even a part of the gospel of the Kingdom that Jesus taught. But, saints, know the Truth, the whole Truth and nothing but the Truth! The Truth will set you free![45]

---

[43] Lk. 6:37: 7 "Do not judge, and you will not be judged. Do not condemn, and you will not be condemned. Forgive, and you will be forgiven.

[44] Lk. 6:37 and Jas. 2:13

[45] Jn. 8:31-38, 44: To the Jews who had believed him, Jesus said, "If you hold to my teaching, you are really my disciples. 32 Then you will know the truth, and the truth will set you free." 33 They answered him, "We are Abraham's descendants and have never been slaves of anyone. How can you say that we shall be set free?" 34 Jesus replied, "I tell you the truth, everyone who sins is a slave to sin. 35 Now a slave has no permanent place in the family, but a son belongs to it forever. 36 So if the Son sets you free, you will be free indeed. 37

The Holy Spirit is moving mightily upon the earth in these end-time[46] days. Even unbelievers are aware of God's judgment coming through the increase of calamities from floods, droughts, earthquakes, hurricanes, tornadoes, volcanoes, hail storms and strong winds.

But believers know that what is happening in the realm of nature is but a minor reflection of what the Spirit is doing in the realm of the Spirit. The natural disasters are God's mercy toward sinners to prepare them to repent and turn to God seeking Him before He sends judgment. Toward believers these disasters are also God's mercy to teach them to trust Him implicitly in all circumstances.[47]

On October 14, 1995, this was reflected in the words the Spirit spoke to me as I journaled:

My son, I am changing the guard, and, yeah, you need to ask Me every day: Where, Lord, do you want me to be today? For I am on the move and you need to know what I am doing this hour! You need to be sensitive to My Spirit and be willing to

I know you are Abraham's descendants. Yet you are ready to kill me, because you have no room for my word. 38 I am telling you what I have seen in the Father's presence, and you do what you have heard from your father." 44 You belong to your father, the devil, and you want to carry out your father's desire. He was a murderer from the beginning, not holding to the truth, for there is no truth in him.

46 Endtime people are those referred to by Jesus as people living after Him. No one knows when the end shall come, but we can know the season. Let him hear who has ears to hear. "But, beloved, be not ignorant of this one thing, that one day [is] with the Lord as a thousand years, and a thousand years as one day." (2 Pet. 3:8)

47 Ps. 41:1,2: Blessed is he who has regard for the weak; the LORD delivers him in times of trouble. 2 The LORD will protect him and preserve his life; he will bless him in the land and not surrender him to the desire of his foes.

move to a new position, to a new place, to a fresh anointing or to a new understanding of what the Spirit is saying to the Church today! Yeah, not to move to a new thing My Spirit is doing shall lead to stagnation and death! Yeah, do not get comfortable in any place or position, for I am on the move! Yeah, and I am replacing people who are not sensitive and who choose to disobey Me, yeah, they choose to fight My Spirit under the guise of doctrine, or tradition, or their interpretation of My word! Yeah, they have all the answers, but they have all the wrong answers, and these are those to whom I shall say: I never knew you!

Yeah, I am pleased with your determination to break through your traditions, your thoughts and your understanding of things to allow Me to make you very sensitive to My Spirit! Yeah, as you continue to yield yourself to My Spirit, I shall mellow you and change you! I shall soften your heart and give you the heart of My Son, Jesus! Yeah, I am changing the guard and some are receiving My anointing with joy and liberty, and I am pleased! Those are the ones I choose to use in these end-times in My mighty endtime work!

I responded in prayer: Lord, I want to have You change my heart, my beliefs, my opinions, my incomplete vision, and I ask You to position me exactly as You desire! I am determined to be used by Your Holy Spirit! I yield to You! Change me so I am a sensitive, willing vessel!

But let me go back to 1987 when the Holy Spirit was beginning to really stir my spirit mightily!

CHAPTER 2

Super Gifts Freely Given

Shortly after we were married, Jean and I went to a Catholic charismatic prayer meeting. This was not a very good first experience for me. A man who stood up and "prophesied" at great length about "little to nothing" turned me off. He was speaking by the flesh and not by the Holy Spirit. I sensed that he was one that loved to hear himself talk. And I was disappointed by the fact that no one in the leadership stopped him or told him to sit down. I do not intend to negate or criticize true prophecy in any way, but many carnal Christians, even those baptized in the Holy Spirit, can and sometimes do operate in the flesh and not in the Spirit.

Needless to say, this experience held me back several years from receiving something every Christian *desperately needs* to live a full Christian life—the baptism of the Holy Spirit. I finally did receive the baptism of the Holy Spirit in 1989 during a prayer meeting which was held in my office. And, oh, what joy I experienced in my spirit.

We can be saved, be baptized in water, have God's life in us and not have our spirit set free from all kinds of bondages. But instead, we can be set free from every constricting stronghold so that we can walk in the authority and the power of God unrestricted and unhindered.

The baptism of the Holy Spirit is what the sacrament of confirmation in most denominations is supposed to be! But no one is set free when a sacrament is used as an instrument to confine and commit people to a denomination instead of inviting the Holy Spirit to set their spirit free. Confirmation instead becomes a stronghold in most denominations rather than freedom to operate in the Spirit. Tradition, man's inventions and legalism pervert blessings which Jesus intended to give us.

The baptism of the Holy Spirit gives us a release of our spirit-man, and that spirit-man begins to be active in speech and action.

One of the first things that happens is the Holy Spirit releases a person to talk to God in another language or to prophesy, just as Jesus' apostles and disciples did on the first Pentecost 2,000 years ago when they spoke in other tongues and prophesied. This is exactly what Jesus promised them.[48] And look what happened when the Holy Spirit came upon them as tongues of fire! They all started speaking in different tongues or prophesying which amazed others standing around observing this event.[49] That was their inner man or their spirit-man speaking to God face to face. What a privilege! What a release! And it is ours for the asking! Just ask the Holy Spirit to come upon you with His baptism of fire and He will not deny your sincere request.

---

[48] Acts 1:4: On one occasion, while he was eating with them, he gave them this command: "Do not leave Jerusalem, but wait for the gift my Father promised, which you have heard me speak about. 5 For John baptized with water, but in a few days *you will be baptized with the Holy Spirit.*" [Italics mine] And in Jn. 16:26: "When the Counselor comes, whom I will send to you from the Father, the Spirit of truth who goes out from the Father, he will testify about me." [Italics mine]

[49] Acts 2:104: When the day of Pentecost came, they were all together in one place. 2 Suddenly a sound like the blowing of a violent wind came from heaven and filled the whole house where they were sitting. 3 They saw what seemed to be tongues of fire that separated and came to rest on each of them. 4 *All of them were filled with the Holy Spirit and began to speak in other tongues as the Spirit enabled them.* [Italics mine]

Many times we do not know how to pray or what to pray for, but when we "pray in the Spirit," that is, we pray in tongues, we are praying the perfect will of God. When we talk or pray by the Holy Spirit, we are talking above and beyond the ability of our mind to comprehend what is being spoken, but our spirit-man knows. In Rom. 8:26,27 it says,

In the same way, the Spirit helps us in our weakness. We do not know what we ought to pray for, but the Spirit himself intercedes for us with groans that words cannot express. And he who searches our hearts knows the mind of the Spirit, because the Spirit intercedes for the saints in accordance with God's will.

Paul said in 1 Cor. 14:2, *"For anyone who speaks in a tongue does not speak to men but to God. Indeed, no one understands him; he utters mysteries with his spirit."* And in 1 Cor. 14:14,15 Paul states,

For if I pray in a tongue, my spirit prays, but my mind is unfruitful. So what shall I do? I will pray with my spirit, but I will also pray with my mind; I will sing with my spirit, but I will also sing with my mind.

What a release of your spirit! Speaking in tongues is one sign that one has received the full baptism of the Holy Spirit, but other signs either accompany or eventually follow, such as words of wisdom, words of knowledge, prophetic utterances, the gift of healing others, etc., as the Holy Spirit chooses.

There are nine major gifts of the Holy Spirit that one can receive.[50] Three are referred to as **word or utterance gifts**: tongues, interpretation of tongues and prophecy. Three are called **revelation gifts**: a word of knowledge, a word of wisdom and discernment of spirits. And three are known as **power gifts**: the gift of faith, of healing and of miracles. There are many other gifts of the Holy Spirit,[51] such as the gift of serving, teaching [or instruction], encouraging, helps ministry [contributing to the needs of others], administration and leadership.[52]

These gifts of the Holy Spirit demonstrate extraordinary endowments of supernatural power operating in ordinary believers. The operation of these gifts are the signs that should be following ordinary believers. Jesus said,

And these signs shall follow them that believe; In my name shall they cast out devils; they shall

---

[50] 1 Cor. 12:4-11: 4 There are different kinds of gifts, but the same Spirit. 5 There are different kinds of service, but the same Lord. 6 There are different kinds of working, but the same God works all of them in all men. 7 Now to each one the manifestation of the Spirit is given for the common good. 8 To one there is given through the Spirit the message of *wisdom*, to another the message of *knowledge* by means of the same Spirit, 9 to another *faith* by the same Spirit, to another gifts of *healing* by that one Spirit, 10 to another *miraculous powers*, to another *prophecy*, to another *distinguishing between spirits*, to another *speaking in different kinds of tongues*, and to still another the *interpretation of tongues*. 11 All these are the work of one and the same Spirit, and he gives them to each one, just as he determines. [Italics mine]

[51] See 1 Cor. 12:28 and Rom. 12:6-8 for an enumeration of others.

[52] Some books that are very helpful in understanding the gifts of the Holy Spirit are: **A** *Handbook on Holy Spirit Baptism* by Don Basham published by Whitaker House, *The Holy Spirit and You* by Dennis & Rita Bennett published by Bridge Publishing, Inc., *Seven Steps to Baptism in the Holy Spirit* by Kenneth Hagin published by Harrison House, and *Overcoming Hindrances to Receiving the Baptism in the Holy Spirit* by John Osteen published by Lakewood Church, Houston, TX.

*speak with new tongues; They shall take up ser-
pents; and if they drink any deadly thing, it shall
not hurt them; they shall lay hands on the sick,
and they shall recover.* [53]

Jesus also said,

*I tell you the truth, anyone who has faith in me will
do what I have been doing. He will do even greater
things than these, because I am going to the
Father. And I will do whatever you ask in my
name, so that the Son may bring glory to the
Father. You may ask me for anything in my name,
and I will do it.* [54]

Imagine, we can **"do even greater things than
these,"** greater things than Jesus did! What a great privilege to
act on behalf of Jesus in our own day and heal and counsel people!

Some church leaders are so afraid of the baptism of the
Holy Spirit that they preach against it. They try to relegate its use
only to the days of the early church, denying that it is needed
now! Could it be that they feel threatened because they cannot
operate in this supernatural miraculous power of the Spirit?
Could that be the reason the gifts are so attacked by some ministers? Are they truly believers if no signs and wonders follow
them?

When a preacher asks, "How many believers are here?"

---

[53] Mk. 16:17,18

[54] Jn. 14:12-14

practically every hand is raised. But then when he asks, "How many have signs and wonders following them regularly?" a couple may be raised.

Satan knows if believers ever recognize their true inheritance as sons of God and heirs of the kingdom, he is in big trouble. So the deceiver does what he is so good at doing, and he uses his tactics of ignorance, doubt, unbelief, fear, deceit, manipulation and control successfully against the leaders to hold back the followers from receiving His gifts! Imagine that! God wants to give us His unlimited power to operate on earth for His purposes and His plan! Oh, we could be so rich if we would only hunger after His righteousness! Jesus said in Mt. 6:33, *"But seek first his kingdom and his righteousness, AND ALL THESE THINGS WILL BE GIVEN TO YOU as well."* [Capitalization mine for emphasis]

Never in history are the gifts more needed than now in the great harvest of souls. **THEY ARE THE EXTRAORDINARY ENDOWMENTS OF SUPERNATURAL POWER OPERATING IN US AS BELIEVERS!** One does not have to be a priest or minister to operate in the power of God! One needs only to be a believer! Supernatural signs shall follow every true believer! Jesus said so! What power He has endowed us with! But we have to be set free first!

Maybe these leaders fear loss of control over God's people and their own programs if they allow the Holy Spirit free reign to operate as He wills. These churches shall become dead churches, full of dead men's bones, just like that of the temple of the Scribes and Pharisees in Jesus' day.[55] Jesus fought these same arguments

---

55 Jesus strongly warns those who are eclectic as to what portion of His word they shall choose to disbelieve simply because it does not fit into their theology

of the Scribes and Pharisees.

But when a pastor and his staff are baptized in the Holy Spirit with His fire, one can see real life abounding, real liberty and joy. And these shepherds will impart the same gifts to their sheep, who will become more than conquerors. Revelation 2:26-29 says,

And he that overcometh, and keepeth my works unto the end, to him will I give power over the

---

or their tradition of man. His gospel does not allow a 'Burger King'® mentality: "Have it your way."™ That's OK for hamburgers, but that's not OK for the truth. We must believe the whole truth and nothing but the truth when it comes to His gospel. In Mt. 23:13 Jesus warns: "Woe to you, teachers of the law and Pharisees, you hypocrites! You shut the kingdom of heaven in men's faces. You yourselves do not enter, nor will you let those enter who are trying to." Those who say prophecy and the gifts of the Holy Spirit were only for the apostolic days of the early church "have a form of godliness but deny the power thereof" [2 Tim. 3:5] and they will not be used by God in the latter days for the great harvest. For the gifts of the Holy Spirit are the tools God will use sovereignly to bring in the great harvest with ease. "'Not by might nor by power, but by My Spirit,' says the Lord Almighty." [Zech 4:6] In Acts 2:14 it says: "Then Peter stood up with the Eleven, raised his voice and addressed the crowd: "Fellow Jews and all of you who live in Jerusalem, let me explain this to you; listen carefully to what I say. 15 These men are not drunk, as you suppose. It's only nine in the morning! 16 No, this is what was spoken by the prophet Joel: 17 "'In the last days, God says, I will pour out my Spirit on all people. Your sons and daughters will prophesy, your young men will see visions, your old men will dream dreams. 18 Even on my servants, both men and women, I will pour out my Spirit in those days, and they will prophesy. 19 I will show wonders in the heaven above and signs on the earth below, blood and fire and billows of smoke. 20 The sun will be turned to darkness and the moon to blood before the coming of the great and glorious day of the Lord.'" Paul advised Timothy in 1 Tim. 2:22-26: 23: "Don't have anything to do with foolish and stupid arguments, because you know they produce quarrels. 24 And the Lord's servant must not quarrel; instead, he must be kind to everyone, able to teach, not resentful. 25 Those who oppose him he must gently instruct, in the hope that God will grant them repentance leading them to a knowledge of the truth, 26 and that they will come to their senses and escape from the trap of the devil, who has taken them captive to do his will." It is my prayer that I can gently instruct those who might otherwise quarrel with the Lord.

nations: And he shall rule them with a rod of iron; as the vessels of a potter shall they be broken to shivers: even as I received of my Father. And I will give him the morning star.[56] *He that hath an ear, let him hear what the Spirit saith unto the churches.* [KJV]

God is in the business of setting captives free, restoring what was lost and making an eternal covenant with His people. This covenant entitles us to have **EVERYTHING GOD HAS** once we give **EVERYTHING WE HAVE** to Him! What an exchange! But that is what covenant is all about! Hallelujah! Thank God that we are covenant people!

To operate *in* the gifts of the Holy Spirit might be likened to steering a sailboat on a smooth lake while sitting back, relaxed, as the Holy Spirit empowers the boat by blowing into the sails. To operate *without* the gifts is likened to paddling a canoe upstream with a pitchfork. Not only does the canoe make no progress, it even goes backward down the stream while the canoer struggles in vain. That is the parallel God wants us to understand in ministering to others. His gifts are our tools for *effective, toiless* ministry! We become vessels and the Holy Spirit becomes the operator with Divine power. No human effort or power can do a Divine job!

Do not grieve the Holy Spirit by saying He doesn't operate

---

[56] The morning star is a visible outward glory of God manifested as a symbol of the hidden, inward purity and holiness. We belong to the King whose kingdom will never end. [Lk. 1:31-33]

[57] Eph. 4: 30: And do not grieve the Holy Spirit of God, with whom you were sealed for the day of redemption.

in and through the Body of Christ today![57]

Do not let anyone deceive you in thinking the gifts of the Holy Spirit are not needed today for the job Jesus has set before us! This job of taking the gospel to the ends of the earth can only be done by divine power operating in humble, human vessels. For 2,000 years the Church has been preaching *the gospel of salvation* with limited success, but Jesus preached *the gospel of the kingdom.*[58] The gospel of salvation is but a tiny part of the gospel of the kingdom. Salvation is only getting to the starting gate, in preparation of being trained to be His disciples, and to run the race to the finish line[59] where we will be crowned with eternal glory! We need the gifts to successfully fulfill the Great Commission—to preach the gospel of the kingdom to the ends of the earth!

It is through the operating in the gifts of the Holy Spirit that Jesus is revealed today to His people, and God gets the glory and honor through the firepower He has given to ordinary believers. As believers, we are able to put faith pressure on the 'super' to change the 'natural.' 1 Pet. 1:6,7 says,

In this you greatly rejoice, though now for a little while you may have had to suffer grief in all kinds of trials. These have come so that your faith—of greater worth than gold, which perishes even though refined by fire—may be proved genuine

---

58 Jesus said in Mt. 24:14: And this *gospel of the kingdom* will be preached in the whole world as a testimony to all nations, and then the end will come. [Italics mine]

59 Heb. 12:1 Therefore, since we are surrounded by such a great cloud of witnesses, let us throw off everything that hinders and the sin that so easily entangles, and let us run with perseverance the race marked out for us.

and may result in praise, glory and honor when Jesus Christ is revealed.

That is putting faith pressure on the super to change the natural.

Simply tell Him of your need and desire for a new out-pouring of His Spirit power and the in-filling of your spirit with the Holy Spirit's fresh fire. It will take you deeper into God. God honors sincere prayer.

The gifts of the Holy Spirit are essential to do Christ's work here on earth the way He wants it done, by the Spirit, rather than by human efforts and good ideas that are not God-ideas. Remember what Abraham did? And Abraham had to wait 13 years before the Lord God even spoke to 'His friend' again after Ishmael was conceived.[60]

Like Abraham, many of us have tried to "help God be God" and help Him do a better job of ruling and reigning over His creation. Many of us have birthed Ishmaels [man's good ideas] rather than Isaacs [God-ideas]. Jesus said: *"The Spirit gives life; the flesh counts for nothing."*[61] To avoid birthing Ishmaels, we need an intimate relationship with the Lord so we can hear Him clearly. *"My sheep hear my voice, and I know them, and they follow me."*[62][KJV]

Therefore let's look at the fruit of the Holy Spirit. That kind of fruit will give us lasting life. *"The words I have spoken to you are spirit and they are life. Yet there are some of you who do not believe."*[63]

---

[60] Read Gen. 16:1 to 18:15 and Gen. 21:1-21

[61] Jn. 6:63

[62] Jn. 10:27

[63] Jn. 6:63b

CHAPTER 3

The Fruit of the Holy Spirit

"But by faith we eagerly await through the Spirit the righteousness for which we hope." [64] And when we speak of righteousness, we are talking about the fruit of the Spirit.

But the fruit of the Spirit is love, joy, peace, patience, kindness, goodness, faithfulness, gentleness and self-control. Against such things there is no law. Those who belong to Christ Jesus have crucified the sinful nature with its passions and desires. Since we live by the Spirit, let us keep in step with the Spirit. [65]

Paul reminds us that we need *the gifts* to minister successfully *to others*. But he tells us we need *the fruit* of the Spirit *for ourselves* lest we be an empty *"gong or a clanging cymbal."* [66] Jesus said: *"By their fruit you will recognize them."* [67]

Does the world recognize you by your fruit either as 1) a follower of Jesus, 2) as a mediocre so-called 'Christian' who scandalizes others and gives them an excuse to continue to live in sin, or 3) as a bed-fellow sinner? You can make the call! God knows the answer. Do you know? Inspect your own fruit and be a good fruit inspector. Jesus said,

---

[64] Gal. 5:5

[65] Gal. 5:22-25

[66] 1 Cor. 13:1

[67] Mt. 7:16

These are the words of the Amen, the faithful and true witness, the ruler of God's creation. I know your deeds, that you are neither cold nor hot. I wish you were either one or the other! So, because you are lukewarm—neither hot nor cold—I am about to spit you out of my mouth. You say, 'I am rich; I have acquired wealth and do not need a thing.' But you do not realize that you are wretched, pitiful, poor, blind and naked. I counsel you to buy from me gold refined in the fire, so you can become rich; and white clothes to wear, so you can cover your shameful nakedness; and salve to put on your eyes, so you can see. Those whom I love I rebuke and discipline. So be earnest, and repent. Here I am! I stand at the door and knock. If anyone hears my voice and opens the door, I will come in and eat with him, and he with me. To him who overcomes, I will give the right to sit with me on my throne, just as I over-came and sat down with my Father on his throne. He who has an ear, let him hear what the Spirit says to the churches." [68]

Jesus hates mediocrity! Mediocrity breeds satisfaction with oneself to the point that pride of life shuts the Holy Spirit out from dealing with that person. And His holiness does not allow unrepentant sin to even come near Him, for God is a consuming fire[69] that burns all that is not holy that comes near! This is time to repent! God will freely give each of us the grace to repent and to

---

[68] Rev. 3:14-18
[69] Heb. 12:29

be right [righteous] with Him.

If we sincerely believe in Him, we must believe His words. Believing His words will lead us to become His disciples. For He said,

> *I am the vine; you are the branches. If a man remains in me and I in him, he will bear much fruit; apart from me you can do nothing. If anyone does not remain in me, he is like a branch that is thrown away and withers; such branches are picked up, thrown into the fire and burned. If you remain in me and my words remain in you, ask whatever you wish, and it will be given you. This is to my Father's glory, that you bear much fruit, showing yourselves to be my disciples."* [70]

A disciple of Jesus is not simply a servant of Jesus, but a friend, for He said,

> *My command is this: Love each other as I have loved you. Greater love has no one than this, that he lay down his life for his friends. You are my friends if you do what I command. I no longer call you servants, because a servant does not know his master's business. Instead, I have called you friends, for everything that I learned from my Father I have made known to you. You did not choose me, but I chose you and appointed you to go and bear fruit—fruit that will last.* [71]

---

[70] Jn. 15:5-8
[71] Jn. 15:12-16

What awesome words from our God!

You see, at just the right time, when we were still powerless, Christ died for the ungodly. Very rarely will anyone die for a righteous man, though for a good man someone might possibly dare to die. But God demonstrates his own love for us in this: While we were still sinners, Christ died for us.[72]

God first loved us while we were still sinners. Thank You, Jesus!

What a demonstration of love! I repeat and capitalize this Scripture so that it will get deep, deep into your spirit!

YOU SEE, AT JUST THE RIGHT TIME, WHEN WE WERE STILL POWERLESS, CHRIST DIED FOR THE UNGODLY. VERY RARELY WILL ANYONE DIE FOR A RIGHTEOUS MAN, THOUGH FOR A GOOD MAN SOMEONE MIGHT POSSIBLY DARE TO DIE. BUT GOD DEMONSTRATES HIS OWN LOVE FOR US IN THIS: WHILE WE WERE STILL SINNERS, CHRIST DIED FOR US. Since we have now been justified by his blood, how much more shall we be saved from God's wrath through him! For if, when we were God's enemies, we were reconciled to him through the death of his Son, how much more, having been reconciled, shall we be saved through his life![73]

---

[72] Rom. 5:6-8
[73] Rom. 5:6-10

Indeed, God thinks more highly of us than we think of ourselves! The reason is if we repent for all sin, we are seen as His very own beloved! The Father sees His Son alive in us, and the Father says, *"This is my Son, whom I love; with him I am well pleased."* [74] *"He hath made us accepted in the beloved."* [75] [KJV]

Look how Paul addressed the saints at Ephesus! Meditate on these precious words and you will know how God sees you!

Blessed [be] the God and Father of our Lord Jesus Christ, who hath blessed us with all spiritual blessings in heavenly [places] in Christ: According as he hath chosen us in him before the foundation of the world, that we should be holy and without blame before him in love: Having predestinated us unto the adoption of children by Jesus Christ to himself, according to the good pleasure of his will, To the praise of the glory of his grace, wherein he hath made us accepted in the beloved. In whom we have redemption through his blood, the forgiveness of sins, according to the riches of his grace; Wherein he hath abounded toward us in all wisdom and prudence; Having made known unto us the mystery of his will, according to his good pleasure which he hath purposed in himself: That in the dispensation of the fulness of times he might gather together in one all things in Christ, both which are in heaven, and which are on earth; [even] in him:

---

[74] Mt. 17:5

[75] Eph. 1:6

In whom also we have obtained an inheritance, being predestinated according to the purpose of him who worketh all things after the counsel of his own will: That we should be to the praise of his glory, who first trusted in Christ. In whom ye also [trusted], after that ye heard the word of truth, the gospel of your salvation: in whom also after that ye believed, ye were sealed with that holy Spirit of promise, Which is the earnest of our inheritance until the redemption of the purchased possession, unto the praise of his glory.[76] [KJV]

God is love and therefore we should love to run in His arms and know the love of the Father.

In this way, love is made complete among us so that we will have confidence on the day of judgment, because in this world we are like him. There is no fear in love. But perfect love drives out fear, because fear has to do with punishment. The one who fears is not made perfect in love. We love because he first loved us.[77]

We can avoid judgment by being in His perfect love and not judging others. *"Judge not, that ye be not judged."* [KJV] *"Do not judge, or you too will be judged. For in the same way you judge others, you will be judged, and with the measure you use, it will be measured to you."* [78] There is a way of avoiding the judgment of God. He has made a

---

[76] Eph. 1:3-14

[77] 1 Jn. 4:17,18

[78] Mt. 7:1,2

way for us sinners! Judge not, and repent!

When Jesus said, *"I counsel you to buy from me gold refined in the fire, so you can become rich,"* He was speaking of being purged through His discipline which is His fire. Jesus was talking about enduring the cross, which is the Lord's discipline to those He loves. His discipline, if received by His disciples, will purify and refine us as pure gold and teach us His ways.[79] When we know God's ways are not our ways, but that His ways are perfect, then we can rest assured no harm will come to us. Rom. 8:28 says, *"And we know that in all things God works for the good of those who love him, who have been called according to his purpose."*

Heb. 12:2-11 says,

Let us fix our eyes on Jesus, the author and perfecter of our faith, who for the joy set before him endured the cross, scorning its shame, and sat down at the right hand of the throne of God. Consider him who endured such opposition from sinful men, so that you will not grow weary and lose heart. In your struggle against sin, you have not yet resisted to the point of shedding your blood. And you have forgotten that word of encouragement that addresses you as sons: 'My son, do not make light of the Lord's discipline, and do not lose heart when he rebukes you, because the Lord disciplines those he loves, and he punishes everyone he accepts as a son.'

---

[79] Rev. 3:18,19

Endure hardship as discipline; God is treating you as sons. For what son is not disciplined by his father? If you are not disciplined (and everyone undergoes discipline), then you are illegitimate children and not true sons. Moreover, we have all had human fathers who disciplined us and we respected them for it. How much more should we submit to the Father of our spirits and live! Our fathers disciplined us for a little while as they thought best; but God disciplines us for our good, that we may share in his holiness. No discipline seems pleasant at the time, but painful. Later on, however, it produces a harvest of righteousness and peace for those who have been trained by it.[80]

We who share in His holiness are not only Jesus' friends, but we are called to be sons of God, heirs of heaven! We can inherit the greatest riches for all eternity by going to the cross for a short time while on earth. What a bargain!

For you did not receive a spirit that makes you a slave again to fear, but you received the Spirit of sonship. And by him we cry, 'Abba, Father.' The Spirit himself testifies with our spirit that we are God's children. Now if we are children, then we are heirs—heirs of God and co-heirs with Christ, if indeed we share in his sufferings in order that we may also share in his glory. I consider that our present sufferings are not worth comparing with the glory that will be revealed in us.[81]

[80] Heb. 12:5-11
[81] Rom. 8:15-18

Oh, what a dignity we have! How God must love us to call us to such a high dignity! And to fulfill and achieve it can be a joy when we pursue the love relationship with Jesus. Remember how your first love affair totally consumed you? Well, Jesus still has that love for you! *"Jesus Christ is the same yesterday and today and forever."* [82]

"I am my lover's and my lover is mine." "I belong to my lover, and his desire is for me." [83]

You and I totally consume His attention. It is similar to what Francis Thompson wrote in his poem, *The Hound of Heaven.* God is the Hound of Heaven pursuing us like a bloodhound on a hot trail "down the labyrinth ways of life." And we run because we fear "lest having Him we should have nought besides." As if having the King of all creation, of both heaven and earth, is nothing at all! Oh, how narrow is our vision at times when we get our focus off of Jesus and on to ourselves! *"God is love!"* [84]

How disappointing it is to realize that many times we forget that we are sons of God.

But you are a chosen people, a royal priesthood, a holy nation, a people belonging to God, that you may declare the praises of him who called you out of darkness into his wonderful light. Once you were not a people, but now you are the people of God; once you had not received mercy, but now you have received mercy. [85]

---

[82] Heb. 13:8

[83] Song of Songs 6:3 and 7:10

[84] 1 Jn. 4:8

[85] 1 Pet. 2:9,10

And we have been called to such a high calling and privileged to worship Him with all our might. For this is the reason we were created—to worship the Lord.

> *Shout for joy to the LORD, all the earth. Worship the LORD with gladness; come before him with joyful songs. Know that the LORD is God. It is he who made us, and we are his; we are his people, the sheep of his pasture. Enter his gates with thanksgiving and his courts with praise; give thanks to him and praise his name. For the LORD is good and his love endures forever; his faithfulness continues through all generations.*[86]

God is a jealous lover. He demands that we put a priority on loving Him. *"Do not worship any other god, for the LORD, whose name is Jealous, is a jealous God."* [87]

This is what the Lord says about Himself in the Scriptures. It must be important to God! For He made a covenant with His people, giving us Himself and all that He is and has in return for our love to Him! He wants to set our hearts on fire for Him! He despises infidelity in us as we despise infidelity in one another.

It is His heart's desire to woo us.

> *When the LORD made a covenant with the Israelites, he commanded them: 'Do not worship any other gods or bow down to them, serve them or sacrifice to them. But the LORD, who brought*

---

[86] Ps. 100:1
[87] Ex. 34:14

you up out of Egypt with mighty power and out-stretched arm, is the one you must worship. . . . Do not forget the covenant I have made with you, and do not worship other gods. Rather, worship the LORD your God; it is he who will deliver you from the hand of all your enemies.' [88]

"Worship the LORD in the splendor of his holiness; tremble before him, all the earth. Say among the nations, 'The LORD reigns.'" [89]

We are talking about the King of kings and the Lord of lords! How awesome is His name! *"He provided redemption for his people; he ordained his covenant forever—holy and awesome is his name."* [90] Lord, give us the faith to have our spiritual eyes opened to see how great Thou art!

Not only is He King and Lord of all, but God is also our loving Father, and we have the privilege of knowing the love of our Father!

As a father has compassion on his children, so the LORD has compassion on those who fear him; for he knows how we are formed, he remembers that we are dust. As for man, his days are like grass, he flourishes like a flower of the field; the wind blows over it and it is gone, and its place remembers it no more. But from everlasting to everlasting the LORD's love is with those who

---

[88] 2 Kgs. 17:35-39
[89] Ps. 96:9
[90] Ps. 111:9

fear him, and his righteousness with their children's children—with those who keep his covenant and remember to obey his precepts.[91]

Please join in agreement with me in this following prayer and allow the Holy Spirit to do a work in both of us!

Lord, I have heeded the counsel You gave in Revelation 3:18-21 to buy from You *"gold refined in the fire"* so I can become rich and wear the white clothes You bestow on us. Please, Lord, cover my shameful nakedness and put salve on my eyes so I can see. Rebuke and discipline me whom You love so I will be earnest and repent. Here I am, too, Lord, in Your presence before You! I hear Your knock on the door and Your voice, and I open the door. Come in and eat with me, and I with You. I choose to be an overcomer, so You will give me the right to sit with You on Your throne, just as You overcame and sat down with Your Father on His throne.[92] Amen!

---

[91] Ps. 103:13-15
[92] Prayer interpolated from Rev. 3:18-21

CHAPTER 4

The Calling and Desert Journey Promised

In early 1987, Jim Partington, an itinerant evangelist from Wales, UK, was visiting in Milwaukee and he was to speak at one of our friends' residence. Jean and I were invited and did attend.

After the meeting, Jim Partington had a prophecy that he spoke over me. In summary, the essence of the prophetic message was:

Amen. Amen. Amen. For the Lord saith: I am preparing you for a new calling. When you were young, honors, awards and recognition were very important to you. But that phase of your life is past.[93] *Now the Lord is about to take you through*

---

[93] While in the active ministry as a priest, I felt like Paul who in Phil. 3:4 wrote: "If anyone else thinks he has reasons to put confidence in the flesh, I have more," for I had received numerous awards, plaques and recognition for my work assisting the mentally retarded and those suffering from alcohol addiction. I was a conscientious priest doing what I was trained to do exactly what Jesus said, "Whatever you did for one of the least of these brothers of mine, you did for me." [Mt. 25:40] Like Paul in Phil. 3:7-9, I today say, "But whatever was to my profit I now consider loss for the sake of Christ. 8 What is more, I consider everything a loss compared to the surpassing greatness of knowing Christ Jesus my Lord, for whose sake I have lost all things. I consider them rubbish, that I may gain Christ 9 and be found in him, not having a righteousness of my own that comes from the law, but that which is through faith in Christ--the righteousness that comes from God and is by faith." Nevertheless, this is my story of that season in my life. One award catapulted me into the limelight, the 1967 FOYM [Five Outstanding Young Men] award from the Wisconsin Jaycees. From then on it seemed like every civic or charitable organization that gave any recognition for public service work wanted to get on the bandwagon and give me an award of recognition. *Outstanding Young Men Of America, 1968 Edition* published my accomplishments.

a valley of financial hardship and bankruptcy to purify you and to prepare your heart for His appointed time when He will lift you up to great heights and bless you abundantly. You are being called to dispense great wealth anonymously for His Kingdom.

I immediately applied this prophecy to my company as the vehicle through which God could use to accomplish the above prophecy. *"For all who are being led by the Spirit of God, these are the sons of God."* [94]   Starting in February, 1988, several men and women who were business people joined me in my office to seek God's perfect will for ourselves at weekly prayer meetings. We opened ourselves to God's purifying fire.

What I did not know then was for my protection, for the Lord was about to lead me into a desert to purge out of me all that was not of Him. Spending time in a desert is not comfortable but it is very necessary in order that the Lord might get our entire attention. The Lord wants us to recognize that we are sons first and servants second! We are heirs of the King and sons of the Mighty God! So I was consoled and encouraged when I recalled the words of Paul regarding sonship in Heb. 12:5-11:

And you have forgotten that word of encouragement that addresses you as sons: "My son, do not make light of the Lord's discipline, and do not lose heart when he rebukes you, because the Lord disciplines those he loves, and he punishes everyone he accepts as a son." Endure hardship as discipline; God is treating you as sons. For what son is not disciplined by his father? If you

---

[94] Rom. 8:14

are not disciplined (and everyone undergoes discipline), then you are illegitimate children and not true sons. Moreover, we have all had human fathers who disciplined us and we respected them for it. How much more should we submit to the Father of our spirits and live! Our fathers disciplined us for a little while as they thought best; but God disciplines us for our good, that we may share in his holiness. No discipline seems pleasant at the time, but painful. Later on, however, it produces a harvest of righteousness and peace for those who have been trained by it.

It is consoling to know that we are not bastards, but heirs—heirs of the Royal King! Hallelujah! And we have royal blood flowing through our veins, for we are temples of the Holy Spirit![95]

---

[95] 1 Cor. 6:19: Do you not know that your body is a temple of the Holy Spirit, who is in you, whom you have received from God? You are not your own; 20 you were bought at a price. Therefore honor God with your body.

Acts 2: 4 *All of them were filled with the Holy Spirit* and began to speak in other tongues as the Spirit enabled them. [Italics mine]

Acts 17:22-30: Paul then stood up in the meeting of the Areopagus and said: "Men of Athens! I see that in every way you are very religious. 23 For as I walked around and looked carefully at your objects of worship, I even found an altar with this inscription: TO AN UNKNOWN GOD. Now what you worship as something unknown I am going to proclaim to you. 24 *"The God who made the world and everything in it is the Lord of heaven and earth and does not live in temples built by hands.* 25 And he is not served by human hands, as if he needed anything, because he himself gives all men life and breath and everything else. 26 From one man he made every nation of men, that they should inhabit the whole earth; and he determined the times set for them and the exact places where they should live. 27 God did this so that men would seek him and perhaps reach out for him and find him, though he is not far from each one of us. 28 *'For in him we live and move and have our being.'* As some of your own poets have said, 'We are his offspring.' 29 "Therefore since we are God's offspring, we should not think that the divine being is like gold or silver or stone--an image made by man's design and skill. 30 In the past God overlooked such ignorance, but now he commands all people everywhere to repent." [Italics mine]

We all have a high calling and a divine destiny, for we are all destined to be priests and kings![96] Hallelujah!

It is in the desert that we come to realize who we are in Christ Jesus![97]

Psalm 63:1-5 expresses the benefits of the desert so well:

O God, you are my God, earnestly I seek you; my soul thirsts for you, my body longs for you, in a dry and weary land where there is no water. I have seen you in the sanctuary and beheld your power and your glory. Because your love is better than

---

[96] Rev. 5:8-10: The four living creatures and the twenty-four elders fell down before the Lamb. Each one had a harp and they were holding golden bowls full of incense, which are the prayers of the saints. 9 And they sang a new song: "You are worthy to take the scroll and to open its seals, because you were slain, and with your blood you purchased men for God from every tribe and language and people and nation. 10 You have made them to be a kingdom and priests to serve our God, and they will reign on the earth."

[97] 1 Jn. 5:20: We know also that the Son of God has come and has given us understanding, so that we may know him who is true. And we are in him who is true--even in his Son Jesus Christ. He is the true God and eternal life. Eph. 2:10: For we are God's workmanship, created in Christ Jesus to do good works, which God prepared in advance for us to do. Phil. 3:7-14: But whatever was to my profit I now consider loss for the sake of Christ. 8 What is more, I consider everything a loss compared to the surpassing greatness of knowing Christ Jesus my Lord, for whose sake I have lost all things. I consider them rubbish, that I may gain Christ 9 and be found in him, not having a righteousness of my own that comes from the law, but that which is through faith in Christ--the righteousness that comes from God and is by faith. 10 I want to know Christ and the power of his resurrection and the fellowship of sharing in his sufferings, becoming like him in his death, 11 and so, somehow, to attain to the resurrection from the dead. 12 Not that I have already obtained all this, or have already been made perfect, but I press on to take hold of that for which Christ Jesus took hold of me. 13 Brothers, I do not consider myself yet to have taken hold of it. But one thing I do: Forgetting what is behind and straining toward what is ahead, 14 I press on toward the goal to win the prize for which God has called me heavenward in Christ Jesus.

life, my lips will glorify you. I will praise you as long as I live, and in your name I will lift up my hands. My soul will be satisfied as with the richest of foods; with singing lips my mouth will praise you.

Such hunger for God increases in the desert as we are led to purification! We become purified by having all iniquity removed as the Spirit shows us. The greater the yielding to the Holy Spirit, the faster the deliverance from iniquity. He must increase so I can decrease.[98]

Listen to the Lord's words to the Israelites when they were in the desert after coming out of Egypt. Though they were out of Egypt, Egypt was not out of them.

Remember how the LORD your God led you all the way in the desert these forty years, to humble you and to test you in order to know what was in your heart, whether or not you would keep his commands. He humbled you, causing you to hunger and then feeding you with manna, which neither you nor your fathers had known, to teach you that man does not live on bread alone but on every word that comes from the mouth of the LORD. Your clothes did not wear out and your feet did not swell during these forty years. Know then in your heart that as a man disciplines his son, so the LORD your God disciplines you.[99]

Our humility determines the time of our wilderness.

---

[98] Jn. 3:30 [KJV]
[99] Deut. 8:2-5

We do not have to be in the desert for forty years just as the Israelites would not have had to be there that length of time. In fact, if they had been ready to obey God, even with the large assembly of three million Israelites and their cattle and belongings, they could have made that journey in eleven days from Egypt to the Promised Land.[100]

But they failed to heed Moses' words:

Observe the commands of the LORD your God, walking in his ways and revering him. For the LORD your God is bringing you into a good land— a land with streams and pools of water, with springs flowing in the valleys and hills; a land with wheat and barley, vines and fig trees, pomegranates, olive oil and honey; a land where bread will not be scarce and you will lack nothing; a land where the rocks are iron and you can dig copper out of the hills.[101]

Indeed, our humility determines the length of time in our wilderness. Like the Israelites, God leads us all the way in the desert—to humble us and to test us in order to [let us] know what is *in our heart*.

To experience God's glory in us we must deal with that iniquity within us! God's glory is His light which cannot co-exist with darkness—the iniquity within! Ask the Lord to show you what iniquity is deeply buried within you so that He will expose it to you and then you can ask Him to remove it!

---

100 Deut. 1:2
101 Deut. 8:6-9

God is faithful and will deliver us from all iniquity! Ps. 103: 1-4 speaks of the iniquity that the Lord wants to remove from us as He increases in us:

> *Bless the LORD, O my soul: and all that is within me, [bless] his holy name. Bless the LORD, O my soul, and forget not all his benefits:* **WHO FOR-GIVETH ALL THINE INIQUITIES**; *who healeth all thy diseases; Who redeemeth thy life from destruction; who crowneth thee with lovingkind-ness and tender mercies; Who satisfieth thy mouth with good [things; so that] thy youth is renewed like the eagle's.* [KJV] [Capital letters mine for emphasis].

I now thank the Lord for my desert experience, *"for to me, to live is Christ and to die* [to self] *is gain!"* [102] *"He must increase, but I [must] decrease."* [KJV][103] Light and darkness cannot exist in the same space! Light always expels darkness, but darkness cannot expel light! Hallelujah! God's glory cannot co-exist with iniquity!

The Lord is preparing His Church as His Bride, without spot and wrinkle or anything of that sort. *"He is coming back for a mature Bride. That he might present it to himself a glorious church, not having spot, or wrinkle, or any such thing; but that it should be holy and without blem-ish."* [104] The King is establishing His kingdom on earth in us! We have been praying for centuries: *"Thy kingdom come. Thy*

---

102 Phil. 1:21
103 Jn. 3:30
104 Eph. 5:25-27

will be done in earth, as [it is] in heaven." [105]

And the Lord is preparing His Bride to shine forth His glory from within for the dark world to see!

> *Arise, shine, for your light has come, and the glory of the LORD rises upon you. See, darkness covers the earth and thick darkness is over the peoples, but the LORD rises upon you and his glory appears over you. Nations will come to your light, and kings to the brightness of your dawn.* [106]

In fact, Paul speaks of the *"mystery hidden for long ages past," "the mystery of Christ"* and *"the mystery of His will"* [107] and this mystery deals with the Bride of Christ. The Bride is the Body of Christ here on earth. It is both Jew and Gentile coming into the kingdom He is establishing in us while we are still here on earth! What an awesome revelation! *"Do you not know that your body is a temple of the Holy Spirit, who is in you, whom you have received from God? You are not your own; you were bought at a price. Therefore honor God with your body."* [108]

Jesus, the Head, has finished His work here on earth as Head that He intended to accomplish; now His work of establishing His kingdom is being accomplished only through Jesus, His Body, which we are! *"So in Christ we who are many form one body, and each member belongs to all the others. We*

---

[105] Mt. 6:10

[106] Is. 60:1-3

[107] Rom. 16:25; Eph. 1:9, 3:3, 3:6; Col. 1:2, 4:3

[108] 1 Cor. 6:19,20

have different gifts, according to the grace given us. He works by His Spirit through His Body!" [109] *"After all, no one ever hated his own body, but he feeds and cares for it, just as Christ does the church—for we are members of his body."* [110]

Jesus is not only perfecting the saints, but He is using us who are ordinary imperfect vessels to perfect other saints under the guidance of the five-fold ministries of apostles, prophets, evangelists, pastors and teachers.

And he gave some, apostles; and some, prophets; and some, evangelists; and some, pastors and teachers; FOR THE PERFECTING OF THE SAINTS, for the work of the ministry, for the edifying of the body of Christ: Till we all come in the unity of the faith, and of the knowledge of the Son of God, unto a perfect man, unto the measure of the stature of the fulness of Christ: That we [henceforth] be no more children, tossed to and fro, and carried about with every wind of doctrine, by the sleight of men, [and] cunning craftiness, whereby they lie in wait to deceive; But speaking the truth in love, may grow up into him in all things, which is the head, [even] Christ: From whom the whole body fitly joined together and compacted by that which every joint supplieth, according to the effectual working in the measure of every part, maketh increase of the body unto

---

[109] Rom. 12:5,6
[110] Eph. 5:29,30

the edifying of itself in love.[111][KJV]

It is through both the fruit and the gifts of the Holy Spirit operating together that we have God's perfect will for our lives. It is the word of God that fills us with divine fruit! There is a saying that if we have the word without the Spirit, we dry up! If we have the Spirit without the word, we blow up! Together with the word and the Spirit, we grow up! The same can be said of the gifts and the fruit of the Holy Spirit. If we have the fruit without the gifts, we dry up. If we have the gifts without the fruit, we blow up. But with both the fruit and the gifts of the Spirit, we grow up! We need both the fruit and the gifts! That was Jesus' intention from the beginning of His ministry on earth, as He demonstrated in His daily walk.

Jesus, full of the Holy Spirit, returned from the Jordan and was led by the Spirit in the desert . . . Jesus returned to Galilee in the power of the Spirit, and news about him spread through the whole countryside.[112]

To some of us, the five-fold ministries are a new concept, though Jesus operated in all five offices. He established and imparted these offices to His apostles while He was on earth. For centuries we have accepted the evangelist, pastor and teacher with no reservations, but somehow we have neglected and even ignored the apostolic and the prophetic offices.

Now Jesus by His Spirit is bringing forth the apostles and prophets to bring the unity in His one true Church which He

---

[111] Eph. 4:11-16 [Capitalization mine for emphasis]
[112] Mt. 4:1,14

prayed for 2,000 years ago.

My prayer is not for them [the 12 apostles] *alone. I pray also for those who will believe in me through their message, that all of them may be one, Father, just as you are in me and I am in you. May they also be in us so that the world may believe that you have sent me. I have given them the glory that you gave me, that they may be one as we are one: I in them and you in me. May they be brought to complete unity to let the world know that you sent me and have loved them even as you have loved me.*[113]

It will be accomplished! *"For the revelation awaits an appointed time; it speaks of the end and will not prove false. Though it linger, wait for it; it will certainly come and will not delay."*[114]

Jesus said: *"Heaven and earth will pass away, but my words will never pass away."*[115]

---

[113] Jn. 17:20-23
[114] Hab. 2:3
[115] Lk. 21:33; Num. 23:19,20; Pr. 30:5,6; Ps. 33:11; Is. 43:13

CHAPTER 5

Iniquity Removed

Iniquity is the root of sin still present within us, that inward motivational force that predisposes us toward sin.[116] It is unconceived sin.[117] Jesus called this iniquity *darkness*.[118] Too long have we been deceived in thinking that this iniquity was us. It isn't us! It's the residue that remains after sin is forgiven and forgotten.

Too long have we carried around in us a heavy load that belongs to the devil, and we have never been paid for carrying that burden! It's time to remove that deceit, wake up and dump off the yoke the devil has laid upon us! What an irony! We were destined to be free, but we were tricked by the devil and not totally delivered from the slavery of sin!

---

[116] Read Rom. 7:14-25, preferably in the Amplified Version of the Bible, to better understand iniquity.

[117] Jas. 1:13-15: When tempted, no one should say, "God is tempting me." For God cannot be tempted by evil, nor does he tempt anyone; 14 but each one is tempted when, by his own evil desire, he is dragged away and enticed. 15 Then, after desire has conceived, it gives birth to sin; and sin, when it is full-grown, gives birth to death.

[118] This mystery of iniquity within us may be addressed at length in a later book; the iniquity is a presence on the inside of us that remains after we have repented and been forgiven of the sin. There is a difference between sin and iniquity. Iniquity is called unrighteousness; Jesus called it darkness. And our soulish nature must gradually be purged of all that iniquity within as the Spirit reveals those things to us that we have struggled with for so many years to overcome. As we yield continually to the Spirit of God, He will purge us step by step, pull out the roots of iniquity, and then allow us to be tested so we can know whether we have totally yielded to His righteousness and seen victory in that area. Do not become discouraged if you fail a test; He will only let you take it over again and again until you pass. See Paul's teaching on this in 2 Thes. 2:7 and Rom. 7:19-24. Owen Johnson has a teaching on iniquity published as a booklet entitled: *Benefits of Blessing The Lord*, Eternal Word Publishing Co., P. O. Box 477, Loris, SC 29569; phone: 803-756-7868.

This iniquity is likened to the grave clothes that Lazarus had wrapped around him when he was laid in his tomb. But Jesus commanded Lazarus, "Come forth!" And He ordered the grave clothes be taken off! Jesus is ordering us to take off our grave clothes! He wants to set us free! Hallelujah! Just get a taste of that freedom and you will never want to go back into bondage again!

The baptism of the Holy Spirit allows us to see this residue of sin that still remains in us after true repentance and salvation. The spirit-man is saved instantaneously when we accept and profess aloud Jesus as the Lord of our life, but the body and the soul are sanctified gradually over a period of time as we yield ourselves to the Holy Spirit. Iniquity must be removed to have God's glory fill us. His glory cannot co-exist with anything unholy. Therefore, we must allow the Holy Spirit to show us what needs to be removed and what habits and mindsets need to be broken. The more we yield to the Holy Spirit, the faster we can be delivered from the iniquity within.

We can remove all barriers that we have grown accustomed to use to protect and even defend that iniquity in the past. How? By discarding our pride in favor of His fire. If we hang on to iniquity when judgment comes and do not let go of the iniquity, we will burn, for the fire of judgment comes to punish all iniquity and anything defending it. Why? Because judgment will expose the truth and burn out all iniquity within us. Judgment is truth exposed and whatever is exposed is being dealt with.

Don't hide the pride any longer. We have been protecting and defending the roots of sin too long thinking it was us! It's not us! It is the residue of sin that the devil uses against us to keep a door open to war against us! All footholds of the devil must go or else the devil is still sitting on his throne within us. *"Do not give the devil a foothold."* [119] As long as the devil has a foothold, he will call on the iniquity within us to defeat us. How can we defeat the enemy when he still resides even a little bit on the inside of us? No army is successful when the enemy is in the camp and knows every secret plan and strategy of attack. It is time to wrestle the iniquity with the help of the Holy Spirit to a complete defeat!

There is an easier way to get rid of that iniquity: just confess your sins one to another and humbly ask for deliverance from them. We will not be judged for what is repented of, for it is then forgotten by God.[120] GOD IS FAITHFUL and will finish what He began in us.[121] *"Therefore confess your sins to each other and pray for each other so that you may be healed."* [122]

The devil's major weapons are fear, ignorance and deception! The Holy Spirit will give us the tools to be delivered. He will bring those things to mind one by one so we can deal with them. Sincerely ask the Holy Spirit to reveal any iniquity within you and repent for allowing it to remain there so long, thus keeping you from being free in the spirit to do God's perfect will for your life. And **THE KEY** to success is to confess it to another brother or sis-

---

[119] Eph. 4:27

[120] Ps. 103: 11-14: For as high as the heavens are above the earth, so great is his love for those who fear him; 12 as far as the east is from the west, so far has he removed our transgressions from us. 13 As a father has compassion on his children, so the LORD has compassion on those who fear him; 14 for he knows how we are formed, he remembers that we are dust.

[121] Phil. 1:6: He who began a good work in you will carry it on to completion until the day of Christ Jesus.

[122] Jas. 5:16

ter!

This is the reason why Christians struggle so long to overcome certain sins even after they are saved and have their spirit sanctified. Anger, pride, lust, impatience, gossip, greed, familiarity, presumption, etc., keep popping up their ugly heads in our daily walk as we struggle—until we deal with that iniquity or that residue of the devil still remaining in our fleshly and soulish realm. The biggest stronghold we have is in our mind, namely, our mind-sets that we are not willing to give up! They have been a part of our lives too long for us to change, or so we think! And the devil keeps reinforcing that stinking thinking! We need to unlearn some things and let the Holy Spirit be our teacher.[123] The gifts of the Spirit are the weapons we need to fight successfully against evil spiritual powers.

The weapons we fight with are not the weapons of the world. On the contrary, they have divine power to demolish strongholds. We demolish arguments and every pretension that sets itself up against the knowledge of God, and we take captive every thought to make it obedient to Christ. And we will be ready to punish every act of disobedience, once your obedience is complete.[124]

---

[123] Jn. 16: 13-15: But when he, the Spirit of truth, comes, he will guide you into all truth. He will not speak on his own; he will speak only what he hears, and he will tell you what is yet to come. 14 He will bring glory to me by taking from what is mine and making it known to you. 15 All that belongs to the Father is mine. That is why I said the Spirit will take from what is mine and make it known to you.

Acts 1: 8: But you will receive power when the Holy Spirit comes on you; and you will be my witnesses in Jerusalem, and in all Judea and Samaria, and to the ends of the earth."

[124] 1 Cor. 10:4-6

Many of us are bound by denominational grave clothes and the Holy Spirit is able to release us and set us free to act like the early Christians did in Acts. To truly worship the Lord, we must allow the Holy Spirit to cleanse us. These early Christians worshipped the Lord in spirit and in truth.

> ***Yet a time is coming and has now come when the true worshipers will worship the Father in spirit and truth, for they are the kind of worshipers the Father seeks. God is spirit, and his worshipers must worship in spirit and in truth.***[125]

His holiness does not allow unrepentant sin to even come near Him, for He is a consuming fire that burns all that is not holy that comes near! Jesus hates mediocrity! Mediocrity breeds satisfaction with oneself to the point that the pride of life shuts the Holy Spirit out from dealing with that person. God's *mercy* wants to triumph over *judgment*, sparing us from any and all *judgment*. But all sin and all iniquity will be dealt with and removed, either by true repentance by ourselves, or by severe *judgment* by God when the season for *mercy* is finished. God cannot deal *mercy* to someone who thinks he has no need for God! But in that case, God will deal *judgment* in its own time! For God is both *merciful* and *just*! This is His time for mercy! Run to Him for His mercy! Don't run away from Him! Run to Him!

It is time to repent for all sin! Forgotten sins do not disappear automatically; each must be repented of to be forgiven. But as they are brought to mind, confessed to another brother or sister in the Lord and forgiven through repentance, those repented sins are removed as far as the east is from the west. ***"For as high as***

---

[125] Jn. 4:23,24

the heavens are above the earth, so great is his love for those who fear him; as far as the east is from the west, so far has he removed our transgressions from us."[126]

And God will freely give each of us the grace to repent and to be right [righteous] with Him.

For God so loved the world that he gave his one and only Son, that whoever believes in him shall not perish but have eternal life. For God did not send his Son into the world to condemn the world, but to save the world through him. Whoever believes in him is not condemned, but whoever does not believe stands condemned already because he has not believed in the name of God's one and only Son.[127]

Sometimes, God uses our enemies and accusers as purging and purifying instruments to cleanse us from all sin and iniquity so we can be holy and manifest the glory of God! How we react to everyday situations tells us whether we are Christlike or influenced by our flesh, the world and the devil. God is our avenger, and He will use our enemies to purge us:

Therefore the Lord, the LORD Almighty, the Mighty One of Israel, declares: "Ah, I will get relief from my foes and avenge myself on my enemies. I will turn my hand against you; I will thoroughly purge away your dross and remove all your impurities."[128]

---

[126] Ps. 103:11,12

[127] Jn. 3:16-18

[128] Is. 1:24,25

The Lord is using these situations as a purification to purge us of all dross so He can rule supremely within us and have His way,[129] just like He did with Joseph in Egypt. And like Joseph, we, too, can proclaim to our brothers, "What you meant for evil, the Lord has meant for good!"[130]

Paul warned Timothy: *"In fact, everyone who wants to live a godly life in Christ Jesus will be persecuted, while evil men and impostors will go from bad to worse, deceiving and being deceived."* [131] And most of those from whom we will encounter persecution are within the Church.[132]

The level of adversity we encounter, however, comes for the purpose of deliverance from all iniquity within, so that we will not be counted among the imposters or phony professing Christians. Not everyone who says: "Lord, Lord," will the Lord Jesus acknowledge as His own: *"Not everyone who says to*

---

[129] Heb. 12:3-11: Consider him who endured such opposition from sinful men, so that you will not grow weary and lose heart. 4 In your struggle against sin, you have not yet resisted to the point of shedding your blood. 5 And you have forgotten that word of encouragement that addresses you as sons: "My son, do not make light of the Lord's discipline, and do not lose heart when he rebukes you, 6 because the Lord disciplines those he loves, and he punishes everyone he accepts as a son." 7 Endure hardship as discipline; God is treating you as sons. For what son is not disciplined by his father? 8 If you are not disciplined (and everyone undergoes discipline), then you are illegitimate children and not true sons. 9 Moreover, we have all had human fathers who disciplined us and we respected them for it. How much more should we submit to the Father of our spirits and live! 10 Our fathers disciplined us for a little while as they thought best; but God disciplines us for our good, that we may share in his holiness. 11 No discipline seems pleasant at the time, but painful. Later on, however, it produces a harvest of righteousness and peace for those who have been trained by it.

[131] Gen. 50:20: You intended to harm me, but God intended it for good to accomplish what is now being done, the saving of many lives.

[132] 2 Tim. 3:12

me, 'Lord, Lord,' will enter the kingdom of heaven, but only he who does the will of my Father who is in heaven."[133] To those not doing the will of the Father, Jesus asked, *"Why do you call me, 'Lord, Lord,' and do not do what I say?"* [134]

Once the iniquity is removed, the reverential fear of the Lord shall increase along with our spiritual discernment so we will be able to clearly see the enemy. Mal. 3:16-18 speaks of those that feared the LORD and spoke

> *often one to another: and the LORD hearkened, and heard [it], and a book of remembrance was written before him for them that feared the LORD, and that thought upon his name. And they shall be mine, saith the LORD of hosts, in that day when I make up my jewels; and I will spare them, as a man spareth his own son that serveth him. Then shall you return, and discern between the righteous and the wicked, between him that serveth God and him that serveth him not.* [KJV]

Read what Paul emphasizes in his letter to Timothy in 1 Tim. 1:15:

> *Here is a trustworthy saying that deserves full acceptance: Christ Jesus came into the world to save sinners—of whom I am the worst. But for that very reason I was shown mercy so that in me, the worst of sinners, Christ Jesus might display*

---

[133] Mt. 7:21
[134] Lk. 4:46

his unlimited patience as an example for those who would believe on him and receive eternal life.

Later Paul re-emphasized that thought to Timothy in 2 Tim. 2:11: *"Here is a trustworthy saying: If we died with him, we will also live with him; if we endure, we will also reign with him."*

God thinks more highly of us than we think of ourselves! And why not? If we repent for all sin and desire to yield to Him to remove all iniquity, we are seen as His very own beloved! The Father looks down as sees His Son alive in us, and the Father says, *"This is my Son, whom I love; with him I am well pleased."* [135] *"He hath made us accepted in the beloved."* [136] [KJV]

Once iniquity is removed, God's glory will manifest itself through us and shine.

Arise, shine, for your light has come, and the glory of the LORD rises upon you. See, darkness covers the earth and thick darkness is over the peoples, but the LORD rises upon you and his glory appears over you. Nations will come to your light, and kings to the brightness of your dawn. [137]

---

[135] Mt. 17:5
[136] Eph. 1:6
[137] Is. 60:1-3

CHAPTER 6

Setting the Stage to Blow Up the Dam: Spiritual Warfare

On Tuesday, June 13, 1989, Evangelist Patti Damus spoke this prophetic word over me:

Thank You, Jesus. I thank you, dear God. Nevertheless God says you are a warrior for Him! In the name of Jesus I come against every spirit of sickness, disease! [138] *All of these restrictions I pray will leave him right now in Jesus' name! I pray for the healing power! I call down for the healing power to flow through him right now in Jesus' name* (Patti prayed in tongues)! *"I have called you to the forefront of the fight," saith God, "and I have armed you with equipment that you know not of! You have been limiting yourself by not expecting more from Me, but I, the Lord your God, will show you even this night the greater works," thus saith the Lord. Hallelujah! Hallelujah!*

Give me your hands, sir! In Jesus' name, anoint these hands that whomever he lays hands on, will be healed! Anoint him with that anointing, in the name of Jesus!

I don't know who you are, but God says you are a

---

[138] At this time I did not know I was ill, but less than two years later it was discovered that cancer had attacked my body for some time.

valiant warrior! And He's giving new and greater strength, equipment, in Jesus' name! Hallelujah! I just saw a helmet of gold put on your head, a warrior's helmet, but it's of gold! Hallelujah! Hallelujah! Praise God! Praise God for that fresh anointing! Thank You, Jesus! Thank You, Jesus!

You have been looking at your infirmities but God says: "Look to Me! For I am doing a new thing in your life, and you will not be the same," saith the Lord, "for your expectation has been enlarged," thus saith God! Thank You, Jesus! Thank You, Jesus! Thank You, Jesus! Thank You, Jesus! Hallelujah! Thank You, Jesus! Thank You, Jesus!

Beloved, do you sometimes feel worthless because of your infirmities? God wants you to know that He sees the stuff that you are made of, and it's not your body. Don't let those things hold you back. He sees your spirit; He sees your heart. He sees your determination to follow Him regard-less. In your sickbed of affliction, you can send armies to Africa. You can dispel the principality and powers over Milwaukee. And as you pray for healing and deliverance for others, you will be healed. God wanted me to tell you that.

Upon my reading this prophecy to a prayer warrior, he commented, "Warriors get wounded, but warriors are leaders, and leaders have followers; and the kind of followers you will have can protect you."

On December 15, 1989, I wrote, *"The Lord said: 'Look at My face, not My hands!'"* *"Not by might, nor by power, but by My Spirit, saith the Lord of Hosts."* [139] In prayer the Lord had been speaking mightily around that time, telling the prayer warriors in our business prayer group that we should step out in faith, that He has placed rocks beneath our feet as we step forward. We were beginning to understand that He has chosen and segregated us to do His work by His Spirit. He has orchestrated our lives accordingly. But we must honor the Lord for who He is, not for what He can do for us! This was a learning process that took some of us years to absorb and put into practice.

On December 16, 1989, Demos Shakarian, founder of Full Gospel Businessmen's Fellowship International, was speaking as a guest of the Milwaukee Chapter. I asked him to personally autograph a copy of his autobiography *"The Happiest People On Earth,"* and in the book he wrote: *"God bless you, Brother Vern. Deut. 28:1-14,"* and shaking his large forefinger in front of my nose, he said prophetically: *"That's for you! That's for you!"* Deut. 28:1-14:

> *If you fully obey the LORD your God and carefully follow all his commands I give you today, the LORD your God will set you high above all the nations on earth. All these blessings will come upon you and accompany you if you obey the LORD your God: You will be blessed in the city and blessed in the country. The fruit of your womb will be blessed, and the crops of your land and the young of your livestock—the calves of*

---

[139] Zech. 4:6

your herds and the lambs of your flocks. Your basket and your kneading trough will be blessed. You will be blessed when you come in and blessed when you go out. The LORD will grant that the enemies who rise up against you will be defeated before you. They will come at you from one direction but flee from you in seven. The LORD will send a blessing on your barns and on everything you put your hand to. The LORD your God will bless you in the land he is giving you. The LORD will establish you as his holy people, as he promised you on oath, if you keep the commands of the LORD your God and walk in his ways. Then all the peoples on earth will see that you are called by the name of the LORD, and they will fear you. The LORD will grant you abundant prosperity—in the fruit of your womb, the young of your livestock and the crops of your ground— in the land he swore to your forefathers to give you. The LORD will open the heavens, the storehouse of his bounty, to send rain on your land in season and to bless all the work of your hands. You will lend to many nations but will borrow from none. The LORD will make you the head, not the tail. If you pay attention to the commands of the LORD your God that I give you this day and carefully follow them, you will always be at the top, never at the bottom. Do not turn aside from any of the commands I give you today, to the right or to the left, following other gods and serving them.

And I firmly believe that is a further confirmation of my

calling! I continue to trust in the Lord with all my heart and lean not on my own understanding; in all things, I acknowledge Him, and He will make my paths straight.[140]

Though I was beginning to realize I was called to be an intercessor, it was a gradual learning process. The devil is not impressed with titles one may hold or the calling one may have. But he knows the authority that Jesus has over him. And just as he answered the seven sons of Sceva, a Jewish chief priest, who attempted to cast out demons, so we had better know the authority we have in Jesus' name and not in our own strength.

The evil spirit stated,

"Jesus I know, and I know about Paul, but who are you?" Then the man who had the evil spirit jumped on them and overpowered them all. He gave them such a beating that they ran out of the house naked and bleeding. When this became known to the Jews and Greeks living in Ephesus, they were all seized with fear, and the name of the Lord Jesus was held in high honor.[141]

Even if we are called to be valiant warriors, we had better recognize that without the anointing, we are simply acting in the flesh. The anointing breaks the yokes over people. **"And it shall come to pass in that day, [that] his burden shall be taken away from off thy shoulder, and his yoke from off thy neck, and the yoke shall be destroyed because of the anointing."[142]** [KJV] This anointing is what gives us new

---

140 Pr. 3:5,6
141 Acts 19:14-16

and greater strength—powerful equipment, in Jesus' name! It is the anointing that breaks the yoke!

We must come to know and believe in the authority and the power Jesus has over satan. So many people who profess to be Christians do not recognize or even believe that satan is real and is influencing evil-minded people to perform horrendous criminal acts.

Look at the mass murders, the tragic genocide Hitler perpetrated on the Jewish people with the cooperation of the German people, the ethnic cleansing taking place today in many, many countries. No human could have that power for evil without the backing of the most murderous spirit, satan himself. It is the master of evil at work through human instruments. The devil can only operate through a physical body that is open to receive his influence. His tools are mediocrity, ignorance and deceit.

My increased awareness of the power of the devil and the great need for intercession was heightened at the North American Congress on the Holy Spirit and World Evangelization in Indianapolis. It was at that five day conference held from August 15 through 19, 1990, that I became more aware of the power of intercession and of the Holy Spirit. The theme was: **EVANGELIZE THE WORLD NOW!** Speakers I heard for the first time at the Conference were men like Bob Weiner, Michael Cassidy, John Wimber, Paul Caine, Bob Jones, Mike Bickle and John Dawson. They had a great impact on my life and set my heart on fire to learn more about spiritual warfare. I came home full of fire for the Lord! As time went on, I began to realize that God was calling and preparing me as an evangelist with a powerful anoint-

---

142 Is. 10:27

ing of intercession. This was a new realization and gave me a new perspective as to what the Lord wanted me to prepare for.

This Congress and the Intercessory Prayer Conference in Minneapolis the following year held from January 31 through February 2, 1991, led by Kjell Sjöberg and Steve Lightle gave me great awareness of satan's strongholds over cities and territories. This was a new concept to me that I never knew or heard preached. In fact, satan has strongholds over churches. This is why churches that have the Spirit of truth and exciting worship services are targeted in an attempt to deaden them by rituals through routine and boring sermons that tend to put one to sleep.

There is a story told of thousands of demons being sent by satan to attend a lively church to distract worshippers from focusing in on the Lord, but only one sleepy demon is assigned to dead churches, and even he falls asleep. There is no work for him to do there.

In Minneapolis I learned techniques and gained knowledge on how to break those strongholds through intercessory warfare! According to Mt. 16:19 we have been given the power to bind and to loose on earth! We must learn to use it!

When we have to face a difficult situation or confront an angry person, we can bind any demons of anger, frustration, hostility, etc., even before we have to confront those spirits in those people. Then regardless whether that demon is possessing or influencing the person, we will be dealing and speaking to a human person instead of a demon spirit on the inside of the person.

Francis Frangipane from Cedar Rapids, IA, conducted a Spiritual Warfare Conference in Milwaukee from October 30 through November 1, 1991. At this Conference, I was asked by an inner city pastor to preach in his church. So on November 22ⁿᵈ I preached a message regarding God's divine destiny for this city and the strong demonic spirits coming against this city's destiny. The message focused on major spirits of religion [tradition], jealousy [racism], competition and control [a Jezebel spirit].

Later that night, we tore down some of those strongholds and pulled some of them up by their roots to destroy their hold over this city. The destiny of Milwaukee as designed by God is to be one of hope for the masses, and satan has attempted to pervert this calling for Milwaukee to be a holy city.

Early in January, 1992, at our office prayer meeting the Lord was telling us to break through, to break forth, step out and claim back the stolen property satan has taken, for *"the thief comes only to steal and kill and destroy"*[143] what is the Lord's![144] Furthermore, *"The weapons we fight with are not the weapons of the world. On the contrary, they have divine power to demolish strongholds."*[145] I wrote: Lord, teach us how to use those weapons! We put you on notice, satan: In the name of Jesus, we claim back all you have stolen from us! Thank You, Jesus! Praise You, Jesus! What a mighty God we serve!

---

[143] Jn. 10:10

[144] Ps. 24:1 The earth is the LORD's, and everything in it, the world, and all who live in it; 2 for he founded it upon the seas and established it upon the waters.

[145] 2 Cor. 10:4

CHAPTER 7

His Prophets Continue to Speak

Another woman evangelist, Edie Roach, with a prophetic gift from Rockford, Illinois, came to Milwaukee on August 7, 1990, and called me out of the audience and spoke a word of knowledge over me:

> *I said that I would do what I promised and I will do it! I say to you: Do not allow the old man to rise up, but put to death the flesh and see your spirit manifest My praise in the midst of what may seem an impossibility. You are My child; I am yours! My Glory will I give to no man. Keep your eyes fixed on the Miracle Worker and not the miracle. I am your Source and I am your Delight. And I will repay all you have sought for and even more! Stand strong and don't be moved by the works of man, but be moved by My hand, for I can move a mountain with the twinkle of an eye. Hallelujah! Thank You, Jesus!*

Then Edie handed me a file card on which, in advance of coming to Milwaukee, she had written a word of knowledge the Lord had given her for me, though she had never met me before. It read as follows:

> *Lay down the things of this world, for they will give you satisfaction for a very short time. I am eternal and your satisfaction in Me will be a permanent thing. I have so much for you to do and it*

is not in the world; it is by My Spirit. I lay before you the things I ask of you and you may choose to follow or to turn to those who know nothing of My Spirit. I say to you: Let your spirit that is within you listen to what I am saying, and then do it. It will bring joy beyond anything you have ever felt before. The world's satisfaction will last a short time and then there is turmoil. Hear me!

Lord, *"your servant is listening. Speak!"* [146]

Another prophetic word over me just charged my spirit and gave me an excitement and joy that the Lord wanted to use me powerfully for His kingdom.

Jim Partington from Wales visited Milwaukee again on November 13, 1990 and had a word for me reminiscent of Is. 40:31 and Deut. 8:18. In summary he said,

The Lord is calling you to another higher level, to greater heights, and you will soar with wings like an eagle, and the Lord will increase and renew your strength, giving you great ability to accomplish His work in the Spirit that He has called you to do. But remember the LORD your God, for it is he who gives you the ability to produce wealth, and so confirms his covenant, which he swore to your forefathers, as it is today.

Jim further added that the work I was called to do is *"not by*

---

[146] 1 Sam. 3:10

might, nor by power, but by My Spirit, says the Lord of Hosts. "[147] After the word of knowledge was spoken, Jim said that the word *"ability"* was impressed on his mind as the important word in this message.

From January 31 through February 2, 1991, Jean and I along with several people from Milwaukee, spent three days in Minneapolis at the Intercessory Prayer Meeting led by Steve Lightle and Kjell Sjöberg of Sweden.[148] The theme was breaking strongholds of satan over our cities. My eyes were opened wide as I realized all that the word teaches us on the authority and power of binding and loosing, breaking curses, both individual and generational curses, and deliverance from demonic influences over our lives! I was beginning to realize and step into my calling as an intercessor. The *"valiant warrior"* in the Spirit as prophesied over me on June 13, 1989, was coming forth:

> *Nevertheless God says you are a warrior for Him! . . . I don't know who you are, but God says you are a valiant warrior! And He's giving new and greater strength, equipment, in Jesus' name! Hallelujah! I just saw a helmet of gold put on your head, a warrior's helmet, but it's of gold! . . . 'I have called you to the forefront of the fight,' saith God, and I have armed you with equipment that you know not of!* [149]

---

[147] Zech. 4:6

[148] Kjell Sjöberg is author of a book on prayer considered a classic: **Winning The Prayer War,** and Steve Lightle is author of **Exodus II.** Other classic books on intercessory prayer can be found in **Appendix B.**

[149] Refer to the chapter: **Setting The Stage To Blow Up The Dam: Spiritual Warfare** for the full prophetic word by Patti Damus.

This was all new but welcome information to me! Why had I never seen this in the Scriptures before now? The blinders were taken off and I praised God for that! Now the fight will be more than even, for we can be assured of victory because we are now able to fight spiritual forces with effective, overpowering spiritual weapons![150] We are more than overcomers! *"In all these things we are more than conquerors through him who loved us."* [151]

---

[150] 2 Cor. 10:4-6: The weapons we fight with are not the weapons of the world. On the contrary, they have divine power to demolish strongholds. 5 We demolish arguments and every pretension that sets itself up against the knowledge of God, and we take captive every thought to make it obedient to Christ. 6 And we will be ready to punish every act of disobedience, once your obedience is complete.

[151] Rom. 8:37

CHAPTER 8

Satan's Attacks Increase

It should go without saying that some prophetic words I have received from a few people were discerned as coming from the flesh of the one speaking it, not from the Spirit.[152] Hence those words were discerned and ignored.[153] Test every spirit!

The enemy will attack only with counterfeits of the real thing. For instance, no counterfeiter prints a $3.00 bill. Therefore, spiritual discernment is paramount and absolutely essential in any walk with the Lord to distinguish true from false prophecies. Paul told Timothy to war over prophetic words spoken over him: ***"Timothy, my son, I give you this instruction in keeping with the prophecies once made about you, so that by following them you may fight the good fight, holding on to faith and a good conscience."***[154]

The higher the calling, the greater the attention paid to that person by the enemy. After the Minneapolis Intercessory Prayer Meeting, many attacks came in various forms of deception, false prophets and temptations to move ahead of God in works of car-

---

[152] 1 Thes. 2:3-11 and Rom. 1:28 discuss the man of sin, the mystery of iniquity and the powerful delusions for those who reject the knowledge of God until He gives them over to a depraved mind to believe the lie.

[153] 1 Jn. 4:1-3: Dear friends, do not believe every spirit, but test the spirits to see whether they are from God, because many false prophets have gone out into the world. 2 This is how you can recognize the Spirit of God: Every spirit that acknowledges that Jesus Christ has come in the flesh is from God, 3 but every spirit that does not acknowledge Jesus is not from God. This is the spirit of the antichrist, which you have heard is coming and even now is already in the world.

[154] 1 Tim. 1:18

nality to "help God be God." A significant book that steered me clear of many pitfalls was *Rees Howells, Intercessor*[155] by Norman Grubb. Though I did stumble time and again while I learned spiritual discernment, I have asked the Lord for that gift continually.

On April 1, 1991, while finishing a business call at a major bank, I felt a severe and sharp pain strike my abdomen much like the piercing of a sharp dagger. I fell to the floor in a fetal position, and with help from my brother, who had accompanied me on the business call, I was helped to the car and driven home. Since the pain did not abate but intensified as time went on, the decision was made to go to the hospital.

The diagnosis was quickly made. There was a large intestinal blockage caused by a huge tumor which had brought the excruciating pain. I was admitted to the hospital for a biopsy. On April 3rd, the results showed the tumor was malignant and would have to be surgically removed immediately. Several doctors came to my room to discuss my options. The doctors thought because of the severe blockage, a colostomy[156] might be the result of surgery.

That evening when the surgeon announced to me that the tumor was malignant, several of our friends who had joined my wife and me to pray in my hospital room, stopped praying as the

---

[155] I highly recommended this book as a classic on spiritual warfare as a life style.

[156] When there is blockage due to a huge tumor in the large intestine, such as was my situation, often a surgical procedure called a colostomy is required, either temporarily or permanently, which in either case creates a situation that is most uncomfortable, very inconvenient and often handicaps free movement about.

surgeon entered my room. We listened to the doctor's report and then immediately continued with prayer and praise. The doctor looked startled and amazed at our joyful response: ***"Praise the Lord, for He is good!"***[157] He left the room quickly with a puzzled look on his face.

Surgery on April 4, 1991, was extremely successful and a colostomy was unnecessary. Praise the Lord! But the doctors discovered that the cancer had already spread to the lymph system and my prognosis for recovery was extremely poor. My situation was very, very serious.

Though I felt I was spiritually ready to meet My Creator and Redeemer, I knew my calling had not been fulfilled and I wanted to do the will of my Father and complete my work here on earth. I knew God has the last word in every matter.

The doctors' opinions gave me little hope for a prolonged life and that poor prognosis was dependent on my receiving heavy chemotherapy treatment for one year.

To say the least, my prognosis was bleak. I was told by the doctors to reduce my work schedule substantially, to about 10% of current activities. This meant I would be forced to close my office in a few months due to a lack of accustomed income from my profession. This later proved to be good advice for I became extremely weak, unable to work full-time and our income spiraled downward. As time passed, I felt the chemotherapy was begin-

---

[157] Nah. 1:7: The LORD is good, a refuge in times of trouble.
Ps. 145: 9 The LORD is good to all; he has compassion on all he has made.
10 All you have made will praise you, O LORD; your saints will extol you.
Ps. 136:1: Give thanks to the LORD, for he is good. His love endures forever.

ning to kill me more than the cancer was.

But this was the beginning of God's way of getting my full attention and separating me from people He did not intend to use to help me fulfill His destiny and calling on my life. I spent long hours on my back speaking to the Lord and listening during the period I was being treated with weekly heavy dosages of chemotherapy.

CHAPTER 9

The Lord's Healing Touch

My hospital discharge was on April 10th and I began chemotherapy on April 24th. Every Thursday morning I went for my intravenous chemotherapy shot and a prescription for chemo pills taken three times a day. With each treatment I could feel the cold chemical running through my veins and I immediately could ascertain that terrible metallic taste.

In the first week of June, I had a business trip scheduled for Denver, Colorado. I had not yet experienced the eventual severe weakness as a result of the chemo treatments.

As the plane was taking off the ground, a lady in her late sixties who sat to my right put her right hand on my shoulder and said to me: "I have a word from the Lord for you!"

I responded with surprise. "Hallelujah! Praise the Lord!," I exclaimed.

She spoke prophetically, *"The Lord told me to tell you that whatever financing you are seeking on this trip, the Lord will provide in His own time. And whatever illness you are suffering from, the Lord will heal miraculously!"*

I asked, "Who are you?" And the lady introduced herself and her husband as deLores and Quentin Clem. I asked: "Where are you from?" She replied, "Escondido, California." In amazement I said, "That's where Merlin Carothers lives." deLores responded, "He's our pastor!" And I declared, "We really have a lot to talk about."

Merlin Carothers is the author of nine different books on the power of praise that I had read and by whom I was greatly blessed. From that day on, I strongly stood on that prophetic word from the Lord, for I knew that my calling and my destiny in this life had not yet been fulfilled. And God is faithful to His word!

Months went by and I became so weak from the chemotherapy that I had to struggle to walk by myself. But, oh, the sweet times the Lord and I had talking to one another as I laid there and counted a million times the many dots on the ceiling.

I spent most of the day either in prayer, reading the word, reading health books or sleeping. I would not trade that time for anything in the world. It was a precious, but trying, time for my faith as well. My faith never weakened. But week by week, I felt my body getting weaker and weaker, to the point I had difficulty balancing and walking by myself. I had to be very cautious while walking lest I fall and seriously injure myself. Sometimes when alone, I crawled to the bathroom so I wouldn't fall.

And I knew that the chemotherapy was killing me, destroying my immune system, the very system I needed to fight the cancer. But I also knew He was going to heal me because He had told me I was called to do several things that had not yet been fulfilled or completed in my life. I was obedient to Him and expected a miraculous healing which I received in His own timing, not my timing. I was being tested severely in my faith. Expect the devil to come against prophetic words spoken because it is his full-time occupation to rob, steal, kill and destroy. He hates to see miraculous healings or healings of any kind. Sickness is from the devil to thwart God's plans for many in this world.

I first changed my eating habits drastically as I learned how to eat healthfully. Reginald Cherry, M. D., has two books out since my cancer that are very good: *The Doctor and the Word*, and *The Bible Cure*, published by Creation House. He also has a series of audio tapes called: *Pathway to Healing Audio Seminar*.

Regarding my eating habits, I learned that our immune system can overcome and successfully beat any cancer or illness if the system is healthy and strong enough. I began juicing fresh vegetables and eating fresh fruit. I practically eliminated all meats or cooked foods, and stayed with fresh uncooked meals, especially fresh salads, fruits and fresh vegetable juices.

Though the chemo made me very weak, especially after each weekly intravenous shot, I managed to keep a good appetite (though everything had a distasteful metallic taste). And I believe the time I had laying on my back in a weakened position at home allowed me to focus on the Lord and praise Him until He answered my Scriptural prayers of healing.

I spoke healing Scriptures over myself again and again and again. I prayed in the Spirit, played praise tapes and read books on praise.

The Lord and I had a good time together because He would not let me become discouraged or entertain any doubt or self-pity! Praise only! No pity! I AM WHO I AM! Praise Me! I am your Healer! I am the All-sufficient One! I am the More-than-enough

One! Praise Me! Worship Me for who I AM! Praise the Lord! I AM WHATEVER YOU NEED ME TO BE!

My business was falling apart and we were experiencing a financial squeeze. While laying on the couch one day, I cried out to the Lord: Help me take care of my family, Lord! And the Lord spoke clearly: ***If you make My business your business, I will make your business My business!*** From that day on the Lord has been running my business. He is my Source!

And I *knew* the Lord was going to heal me miraculously. When I heard the news that Evangelist Patti Damus was returning to Milwaukee to minister, I knew I had to be present for the meeting.

On Tuesday and Wednesday evenings, September 17 and 18, 1991, Patti Damus was in town at Pipeline to Jesus Prayer Group. I went forward both nights and she had a word of prophecy for me. I told her I had surgery for cancer in April and was undergoing chemotherapy, but I felt I'm on my way to recovery, though the heavy doses of chemotherapy were causing me to become extremely weak. The first night she had a prophetic prayer of healing.

Patti prayed,

Lord, I thank You for this life. Thank You, Jesus. I thank You for giving him life. I pray, Lord, for a total healing from cancer, that there be no after-effects, that there be no re-occurrence. I cancel out all cancer from this body in Jesus' name. I pray that You will rejuvenate him; he'll be stronger

than ever, stronger than he has ever been in his life, that he will be a living testimony for You, dear God, that You will anoint his tongue. You will anoint the words to be spoken through him. Thank You, Jesus. Thank You, Jesus! Praise God!

God is going to use you as a spokesman for the mighty miracle-power of God! He's going to use you as a spokesman for the mighty miracle-power of God! He's going to use you as a spokesman. I can see you before a people, a crowd—God is speaking! God is speaking through you—and you're sharing the love of God! Praise God! Hallelujah! God loves you!

Immediately I received great strength and energy through-out my body and I felt like dancing all night. I *knew* I was healed *instantaneously* because my strength and vigor returned. I came home, danced through the living room and announced to my wife that I am stopping my chemotherapy immediately because the Lord had healed me miraculously! Praise God! I felt as if I were living out the word of the Lord which the prophet Malachi described in Mal. 4:2: *"But for you who revere my name, the sun of righteousness will rise with healing in its wings. And you will go out and leap like calves released from the stall."* Hallelujah! Praise the Lord!

The second night I asked for prayer to heal my left knee injury and to release the gifts of the Holy Spirit. Patti prayed,

Lord, I pray for a complete and total healing of

that left knee in Jesus' name; I pray that you will reconstruct it, reconstruct that left knee; totally heal it! And, Lord, I pray that you will stir up all the gifts of the Spirit, and cause them to operate, cause them to manifest! Lord, just give him a special anointing of the Holy Spirit and stir up those gifts, and bring them, bring them up, bring them out, to be manifested, in Jesus' name! Hallelujah! Hallelujah! Hallelujah!

He is giving you like the heart of an evangelist and you're going to be sharing in a new fresh way, at ease. Sometimes you wanted to share in the past and you didn't share at ease. You're going to be sharing with greater ease. Thank You, dear God! Hallelujah! Hallelujah! Thank You, God! Praise God!

I knew my healing was definitely connected with my calling which now is being fulfilled: ***"God is going to use you as a spokesman for the mighty miracle-power of God! . . . He is giving you like the heart of an evangelist and you're going to be sharing in a new fresh way, at ease."*** My calling as an evangelist and as a spokesman for His miracle-working power has been growing stronger in my spirit.

Its full manifestation, however, is in God's timing; I await His initiation of that calling in its fullness. Like the men of Issachar, who understood the times and knew what Israel should do, so we must also know God's timing for everything.[158] It is a hard but necessary lesson we all need to learn, because if anything

---

[158] 1 Chron. 12:32

is done out of His timing, God is not in it. Then it is just human will power instead of divine power at work. Another way that Ishmaels are birthed is by being out of God's timing.

On Thursday mornings, I went for my regularly scheduled weekly intravenous chemo injection and chemo pills at the office of my oncology physician. This Thursday, however, before I allowed them to draw a blood sample, I requested to speak to my doctor. When I shared with him that I was healed miraculously on Tuesday night and was stopping all chemotherapy treatment, he looked surprised and puzzled, and said, "I can't recommend what you are doing, but I will respect your decision and will work with you." He requested that I come for regular follow-up visits; when I consented, then he asked if he could draw a blood sample.

After analyzing the blood sample, my doctor commented, "Oh, I see you have been taking heavy dosages of iron pills!" I told him I've never taken any iron pills. He scratched his head and said, "With the kind of exposure you've had to chemotherapy it usually takes a full year of heavy dosages of iron pills to get your iron level back to normal; but your iron level is normal now." I responded: "Doc, God doesn't do a half job when he heals!" Praise God!

To the believer, no proof of a miraculous healing is necessary; to the unbeliever no proof is sufficient! One can only plant seeds into other people's lives and it's up to them to receive or reject them.[159]

---

159 Those looking to the Lord for healing need to proclaim daily over themselves healing Scriptures. Some of those words I typed up and proclaimed in faith to sow them deep within my spirit are found in **Appendix C** in the back of the book.

At that time, the Lord had been telling us to enlarge our expectations beyond our wildest dreams as to what He is calling us to do, because He is doing His mighty work through us **"by His Spirit."** [160] We are to enlarge our expectations regarding the great calling to feed His people worldwide during the coming trials of these endtimes. We must focus on Him! **"Let us fix our eyes on Jesus!"** [161]

And to fulfill that enlarged calling of the Lord we need perfect health.

On Wednesday, March 11, 1992, I went for my regular physical check-up and my oncologist admitted all signs were excellent; I was able to witness to a nurse about the mighty power and miraculous work of God in my life. Praise God! At that time, I convinced the oncologist that I did not need to return to the oncology department for at least three months. My oncology physician was satisfied that there were no signs of any cancer, though he was cautiously observant, as his training might require, but quite unnecessary for those convinced that a miracle had taken place.

At the next follow-up visit, I urged him to schedule only semi-annual visits, then after that only an annual visit. At my fourth year anniversary check-up, my doctor finally admitted that he knew of no other explanation for my instant healing and ongoing recovery except divine intervention. I thanked him for his services and told him that if he wanted to see me on my fifth anniversary, he would have to pay me to come in, instead of me paying the doctor. I never heard from him after that.

---

[160] Zech. 4:6

[161] Heb. 12:2

About six years after the surgery, the surgeon phoned me; he was retiring from his practice as chief surgeon at a major hospital and said there were few patients in his career that stood out so vividly in his memory, and I was one of them. He wanted to see me and queried me about my positive outlook toward cancer and my confidence in recovering from it. I witnessed to him regarding my faith in the miraculous healing power of God, and said, "My destiny was not fulfilled! So God intervened."

Needless to say, I am in great health today, not only because of **Divine Healing**, but I am believing for **Divine Health** where no attack or sickness can ever touch me again! There is a big difference between the two. To maintain Divine Health, I watch my diet closely, though I do eat some meat [mostly chicken, some beef, no pork] and I have gone to see Dr. Judy Seeger, N. D., a naturopathist who is a Christian that operates the River of Life Health Center in Green Bay, Wisconsin. She put my wife and me on a program that keeps us lively and healthy.

At the time of this writing, I am 66 years old and feel like I'm 33. I have energy today that makes young people wonder where I get it all! *"The Lord is my helper; I will not be afraid!"* [162] *"The joy of the Lord is my strength!"* [163] These Scriptures have become reality in my life!

Also, I encourage people, both sick and healthy, to plead the Blood of Jesus over themselves every morning! There's power in the Blood![164] My wife and I anoint each other every morning we are together and plead the Blood of Jesus over each other.

---

162 Heb. 13:6 and Ps. 118:6,7
163 Neh. 8:10
164 Heb. 2:14,15

CHAPTER 10

By Their Fruit You Will Know Them

The devil knows when God is moving and calling people to do His will. He uses other Christians who do not know the Father and cannot hear clearly from God or have less than pure motives in their enthusiasm to serve God. Jesus even warned us about such people:

> **When the Counselor comes, whom I will send to you from the Father, the Spirit of truth who goes out from the Father, he will testify about me. And you also must testify, for you have been with me from the beginning. All this I have told you so that you will not go astray. They will put you out of the synagogue; in fact, a time is coming when anyone who kills you will think he is offering a service to God. They will do such things because they have not known the Father or me. I have told you this, so that when the time comes you will remember that I warned you.**[165]

Just imagine! This is not a figment of Jesus' imagination. He stated this as *fact!* **"In fact, a time is coming when anyone who kills you will think he is offering a service to God."**

Exactly one month to the day after my miraculous healing, an event took place that I thought was instigated by the Lord. Let

---

[165] Jn. 15:26-16:4

me share this and a couple other stories as examples which I experienced that were worthy lessons to teach me the need for great wisdom and discernment. Wisdom is needed to know when and to whom to speak and when not and to whom not to speak. Discernment is needed to know the heart of a man by the Spirit. In World War II the saying was coined: Loose lips sink ships!

On October 17, 1991, a businessman, whom we will call George, and his wife came to town. I was introduced to them by a brother whom I perceived as credible, had breakfast with them and then we prayed together. As we prayed, I sensed the Lord was speaking to me: *We are to enlarge our expectations as to the great calling and blessing He is engineering through the Company and that we will be feeding His people worldwide during the coming trials of these endtimes.*

We must focus on Him! *"Let us fix our eyes on Jesus."*[166] If our eyes get off of Jesus, we can be deceived easily and may never know it for months to come.

Jesus warned us,

Watch out for false prophets. They come to you in sheep's clothing, but inwardly they are ferocious wolves. By their fruit you will recognize them. Do people pick grapes from thornbushes, or figs from thistles? Likewise every good tree bears good fruit, but a bad tree bears bad fruit. A good tree cannot bear bad fruit, and a bad tree cannot bear good fruit. Every tree that does not bear

---

[166] Heb. 12:2

good fruit is cut down and thrown into the fire. Thus, by their fruit you will recognize them.[167]

On October 21, 1991, I had lunch with a prophetic lady who shared that she had a vision two years ago and was just now released to share it with me: *I was standing and preaching to crowds of many nations. It was as if I, as the head of my company, was the spiritual leader of an international company, made up of employees from many different nations, which was influencing the whole world in feeding His people, preaching the word and sharing the riches of God. She saw that my company will be led to many countries to major resources to be used for His Kingdom.*

I thought that this prophetic word by this lady was timed by the Lord to be released to me as a confirmation to work with this businessman. Everything seemed as though it was falling into place without me attempting to orchestrate anything.

However, I had not seriously taken this to the Lord for true discernment. I relied on the opinion of others whom I respected. But Jesus gave us further warning regarding with whom we are to be associated:

Many will say to me on that day, "Lord, Lord, did we not prophesy in your name, and in your name drive out demons and perform many miracles?" Then I will tell them plainly, "I never knew you. Away from me, you evildoers!" Therefore everyone who hears these words of mine and puts them into practice is

---

[167] Mt. 7:15-20

like a wise man who built his house on the rock. The rain came down, the streams rose, and the winds blew and beat against that house; yet it did not fall, because it had its foundation on the rock.[168]

I was not like the wise man who built his house on the rock. Therefore, I inherited the consequences. *"But everyone who hears these words of mine and does not put them into practice is like a foolish man who built his house on sand. The rain came down, the streams rose, and the winds blew and beat against that house, and it fell with a great crash."* [169]

I had been foolish. Essentially, because of this distraction, I lost one good year of time—a year that I desperately needed to rebuild my business after the devastating losses I had incurred during the months I was ill and undergoing the chemotherapy. My business had begun to dry up, leaving me with about half of my clientele.

I had opened a portion of my office to two of George's people who worked for him. After about a year, when I was forced to leave the office because of my inability to stay current with my financial obligations, I was overwhelmed to find that I was "left holding the bag" for a huge telephone bill with hundreds of international and national lengthy long distance phone calls as well as several months of unpaid back rent. It was a time that I could ill afford to take on the liabilities of others when I was incapable of handling my own.

---

168 Mt. 7:22-25
169 Mt. 7:26,27

This turned me to the Lord for wisdom and discernment. And I clearly saw the wolf in sheep's clothing. After you have dealt at length with a false prophet, it is easy to recognize a true one. The Lord allowed this experience at a time in my life, not so that it would devastate me, but to prepare me for my future ministry.

Jim Partington, a truly prophetic and godly person, ministered in Milwaukee again on October 29, 1991, and had this encouraging prophetic word for me:

Amen. For the Lord thy God shall increase thy vision; thou shall see more clearly. Thou shall understand with a greater understanding than thou hast ever had before, for thy God shall be thy eyes! Thy God shall give thee visions, and thou shall see things, and thou shall speak what thou dost see! I will show thee My hidden treasures, saith the Lord thy God. Thou shall not seek out; thou shall not pry; thou shall not discover, but I shall give—freely. Amen.

The Lord opened my eyes wide and I saw that the flowery expressions of prayer and Biblical counsel from George were nothing but a con artist's slick Bible talk in a scheme to get something for nothing. I thank the Lord that I wasn't working any closer with him during that time, though I was invited to do so. The Lord did have His ministering angels watching over me so that I was not hurt beyond recovery.

This man proved to be as phony as a three-dollar bill, though he said all the right things. By *"their fruit you shall know them."* [170] It was a great lesson in discernment.

In the past, the greatest mistake I have made in business was getting involved with the wrong people. Because of my failure to step back and seek the Lord for discernment of the truth, I had to bear the consequences and pay the price.

On New Year's Day, 1992, a friend advised me to try every spirit to see if it be of God in every case:

> *Dear friends, do not believe every spirit, but test the spirits to see whether they are from God, because many false prophets have gone out into the world. This is how you can recognize the Spirit of God: Every spirit that acknowledges that Jesus Christ has come in the flesh is from God, but every spirit that does not acknowledge Jesus is not from God. This is the spirit of the antichrist, which you have heard is coming and even now is already in the world.* [171]

I prayed: Lord, give me discernment of spirits! Hallelujah!

Another unwelcome situation arose even before this first one was resolved. On March 19, 1992, I had a "Job experience" [172] when three well-meaning but misinformed and misguided Christian businessmen visited my office to correct me and reprove me for sharing my vision with others. They implied I was deluded and involved in some illegal activity. I told them I could not share their viewpoint, nor would they share mine, but I would be very careful to whom I would speak from this day forward. I

---

[170] Mt. 7:20

now know how Job felt having "his friends" advising him.

But this is the attitude we are to have when we are persecuted: ***"Consider it pure joy, my brothers, whenever you face trials of many kinds, because you know that the testing of your faith develops perseverance. Perseverance must finish its work so that you may be mature and complete, not lacking anything."*** [173]

Only God truly knows the hearts of men.[174] Like Job, I prayed for these men[175] and I hold no bitterness or unforgiveness towards any accuser. Jesus told us to pray for our enemies; do good to them.[176] And I repented of any misgivings or misrepresentations! Praise God! But I will obey God rather than men!

---

[171] 1 Jn. 4:1-3

[172] Read the book of Job and the unwise advice and accusatory statements made to this just man by "his friends."

[173] Jas. 1:2-4; other Scriptures regarding persecution are: 2 Tim. 3:12: In fact, everyone who wants to live a godly life in Christ Jesus will be persecuted, and Ps. 64:1-4: Hear me, O God, as I voice my complaint; protect my life from the threat of the enemy. 2 Hide me from the conspiracy of the wicked, from that noisy crowd of evildoers. 3 They sharpen their tongues like swords and aim their words like deadly arrows. 4 They shoot from ambush at the innocent man; they shoot at him suddenly, without fear.

[174] 1 Kgs. 8:39,40: ...and when a prayer or plea is made by any of your people Israel--each one aware of the afflictions of his own heart, and spreading out his hands toward this temple-- 39 then hear from heaven, your dwelling place. Forgive and act; deal with each man according to all he does, *since you know his heart (for you alone know the hearts of all men).* [Italics mine]

[175] Job 42:10

[176] Mt. 5:44-48: But I tell you: Love your enemies and pray for those who persecute you, 45 that you may be sons of your Father in heaven. He causes his sun to rise on the evil and the good, and sends rain on the righteous and the unrighteous. 46 If you love those who love you, what reward will you get? Are not even the tax collectors doing that? 47 And if you greet only your brothers, what are you doing more than others? Do not even pagans do that? 48 Be perfect, therefore, as your heavenly Father is perfect.

And I will seek His counsel!

I believe the above described incidents are but a beginning of what we may expect, when according to Revelations 12:10, the *"accuser of the brethren"* will use members of the Body of Christ to come against those whom He has chosen to do His perfect will! *"Our struggle is not against flesh and blood, but against the rulers, against the authorities, against the powers of this dark world and against the spiritual forces of evil in the heavenly realms."* [177] We are not fighting people but the demons controlling people, and we cannot win a spiritual battle with carnal weapons; they have no effect whatsoever. So we need to do spiritual warfare with spiritual weapons to defeat the enemy and become overcomers! [178] We have to stop fighting people and start fighting the demonic forces manipulating and controlling people.

The Lord will then tell us like He did David and the Israelites who had sought the Lord: *"The battle is the Lord's"* [179] David's story is found in 1 Sam. 17:45-47 where he fought the spirit controlling the uncircumcised Philistine giant. David spoke boldly to Goliath and all the Philistines who defied the armies of the living God:

> *Then David said to the Philistine, "You come against me with sword and spear and javelin, but I come against you in the name of the LORD*

---

[177] Eph. 6:12

[178] Ps. 144:1,2: Praise be to the LORD my Rock, who trains my hands for war, my fingers for battle. 2 He is my loving God and my fortress, my stronghold and my deliverer, my shield, in whom I take refuge, who subdues peoples under me.

[179] 1 Sam. 17:47

Almighty, the God of the armies of Israel, whom you have defied. This day the LORD will hand you over to me, and I'll strike you down and cut off your head. Today I will give the carcasses of the Philistine army to the birds of the air and the beasts of the earth, and the whole world will know that there is a God in Israel. All those gathered here will know that it is not by sword or spear that the LORD saves; for <u>the battle is the LORD's</u>, and he will give all of you into our hands."

Later David wrote about this in a psalm, saying, *"But you are a shield around me, O Lord; you bestow glory on me and lift up my head."* [180]

This story of David and Goliath teaches us that the giant had a bigger house, but a little spirit was inside. David had a little house but a giant Spirit was on the inside of little David. And God was on David's side and protected him.

Often when God uses our accusers as a purging and purifying instrument to cleanse us from all sin and iniquity, we can become holy and manifest the glory of God at a more quicker pace! How we react to everyday situations tells us whether we are Christlike or un-Christlike.

Jesus is our model on the cross, *"Father, forgive them, for they do not know what they are doing."* [181]

The very day that the "accusers" had come to see me, a

---

[180] Ps. 3:3
[181] Lk. 23:24

strong anointing descended upon me about 5:15 P.M. while I was alone in the office. I stopped typing and sat in His presence, waiting for the Lord to speak. After about ten minutes He said regarding the three well-intentioned but misguided "brothers:" *I will speak to you whenever you are accused. Be at peace!*

I waited about another five minutes when the Lord said, regarding another matter of concern *"Do not be concerned; I am a mighty warrior; you haven't seen Me in battle yet!"* Praise God!

I thought of two Scripture passages: *"For the battle is not yours, but God's,"* [182] and, *"Who is this King of glory? The LORD strong and mighty, the LORD mighty in battle."* [183]

While reading *Holiness, Truth and the Presence of God* by Francis Frangipane, I was impressed by these words on page 56: "Christians, who tend to automatically assume they are the *'chosen of God,'* have reassured themselves that they could not possibly be deceived. The very thought, 'I cannot be deceived' is itself a deception! Let us stay humble and not presume that the calling of God and the choosing of God are alike. *'Many are called,'* Jesus taught, *'but few are chosen.'"* [184]

Many tests await the called before they are equipped by God and become His chosen, not the least of which is becoming free from deception through the purifying fire. *"And this gospel of the kingdom (the whole message of Jesus Christ) will be preached in the whole world as a testi-*

---

[182] 2 Chron. 20:15

[183] Ps. 24:8

[184] Mt. 22:14

mony (witness) to all nations"[185] before His return.[186]

And Jesus answered and said unto them, Take heed that no man deceive you. For many shall come in my name, saying, I am Christ; and shall deceive many. And ye shall hear of wars and rumours of wars: see that ye be not troubled: for all [these things] must come to pass, but the end is not yet. For nation shall rise against nation, and kingdom against kingdom: and there shall be famines, and pestilences, and earthquakes, in divers places. All these [are] the beginning of sorrows. Then shall they deliver you up to be afflicted, and shall kill you: and ye shall be hated of all nations for my name's sake. And then shall many be offended, and shall betray one another, and shall hate one another. And many false prophets shall rise, and shall deceive many. And because iniquity shall abound, the love of many shall wax cold. But he that shall endure unto the end, the same shall be saved. And this gospel of the kingdom shall be preached in all the world for a witness unto all nations; and then shall the end come.[187][KJV]

Endurance is outlasting the devil. Remember, the devil is a short-term skirmisher. Perseverance and faithfulness will outlast the devil.

---

185 Mt. 24:14

186 Jesus is coming back [not for a sickly immature little flower girl but] for a mature Bride, without spot or wrinkle or anything of that sort as it says in Eph. 5:25-27; Rev. 19:7,8; 21:2, 9; 22:17; a Bride that will be priests of God and of Christ and will reign with Him for a thousand years as it proclaims in Rev. 20:6.

187 Mt. 24:4-14

122

CHAPTER 11

The Power of Praise

All Christians are praying for revival and renewal to come upon the face of the earth! True revival is a turning around, doing a 180° turn, an about-face back toward what we should have been doing all along. Dr. Michael Brown, the Director of the Brownsville Revival School of Ministry in Pensacola, Florida, defines revival as "the season of unusual divine visitation resulting in deep repentance, supernatural renewal and sweeping reformation in the Church, resulting in the radical conversion of sinners in the world after producing moral, social and economic change in the local and national communities."[188]

One of the most powerful and effective tools to bring about revival upon the earth is praise! Read the prophetic word on the power of praise as spoken on February 19, 1994, by Burton Seavey in Oak Park, IL, at The School of The Holy Spirit. Burton spoke,

And the Lord does speak to His people even this hour, and will tell you of the power that is in praise! And I will assure you, My children, that this year I will begin to reveal to you the awesome power that is contained in praise! For hitherto the Church has thought of praise as being simply an expression of one's lips and voice to Me, the Almighty God, in telling Me how great I am! Indeed, it is that! But it is far more than that! For

---

[188] Delivered in a sermon to leaders in Brownsville Assembly of God Church on April 23, 1999.

there is intrinsic power that I have invested in the praises of My people!

Did I not oftentimes in days gone by send the praisers out even ahead of the ark, even ahead of the armies, and as they praised Me, the power of the heavens was loosed, and the enemy fell before them as though they were nothing.

Yet you go about in the doldrums; you go about in the blues, and go about in your hard times. You go about in your pains; you go about in your difficulties; you go about in the hard times and all of the distresses of life pile up on you. And you speak about them, and you talk about them, and you invest power in them by your words!

But I, the Lord your God, want to release you into a new dimension of knowing Me, that when those times come up before you, as a strongman, dressed in armor, you will not fight back in your own strength! You will not invest power in them by speaking about how awesome they are!

You will begin to praise Me, saith the Lord! You will lift your voice in glory to Me! And in that hour you will watch that strongman's armor begin to crumble into little pieces, and fall at his feet and dissolve into nothingness! And underneath you will see the scrawny little impotent creature that he really is!

He hides behind the awesomeness of that which scares you and frightens you! But I will bring him down! And I will make him bow at your feet and recognize that the Christ in you is Lord of glory!

I will bring your difficulties down; I will bring your troubles down; I will bring your heartaches down; I will bring your distresses down; I will bring your financial difficulties down; and I will lay them at your feet, as a defeated strongman! And you will walk up and put your feet on the neck of that one that troubled you so. And you will know the feel of victory, for I am raising up a company of people filled with power, filled with glory, filled with signs, filled with wonders, and I will lead you forth in My power!

And there is no power that can stand before you! For if God be for you, who can be against you? No weapon that is formed against you shall prosper, if you will only praise Me, saith the Lord! Hallelujah! Hallelujah! Hallelujah!

And everyone shouted: Praise You, Lord! Praise God! Praise Him! Hallelujah! Praise God! We praise You! Glory, glory, glory!

Then Burton Seavey said, "Hallelujah! What a powerful word! What a powerful word! Not because I gave it; I don't mean that, but just because I knew God is trying to speak to the Church about something that maybe we don't understand! And that is just what He said! There is an awesome power in praise! If you begin to release it, you are going to see God move in your life in a new dimension that you've never seen before! Hallelujah!"

Then after prophetic words for several individuals, one of the prophets had a word that seemed to apply to non-praisers who did not understand the power in praising God,

This is a general word to the body the Lord is sharing with me:

We need to be tough on the inside, especially now! A tender heart towards God and people, but being tough on the inside! Because as the persecution comes, the enemy is going to begin to do his lying signs and wonders!

And if the believers are not doing the signs and wonders of God, as the Holy Spirit works through them, it's going to mislead the lost and mislead those who don't know the word to the enemy. And that there are people that still aren't even sure that the prophetic is of God yet! And it's time to grow up! And it's time to recognize that God's word is forever!

The things that were done in the Acts are for now just as they were for then. As the persecution heats up, which it will, God's power heats up also!

And He needs willing vessels, willing to take a stand and there are people I saw; we were talking at breakfast a little about the war going on in the

Middle East, but the Lord showed me here, that some people are like in a fox hole, covered up with dirt, because the enemy was shelling their life with emotional pains and ridicule, criticisms even from their youth, even sexual abuse and emotional abuse. And so, those are just buried, afraid to go up!

But you can't take the land unless you get out of the fox hole, and get in an offensive position, instead of just having your hands spiritually over your head just hoping not to get hurt anymore!

And God will begin to heal us as we begin to move in His call! And I just know that there are people who will recognize their call today. It's going to become clear.

And God can't wait too much longer for some folks, even in this room! It's like He's been dealing with you, dealing with you, dealing with you! And pretty soon if you don't start moving, He is going to have to get somebody else to get the job done! He doesn't want any of His children, any people lost, because we don't want to move!

The power of praise should never be discounted in our prayer life. Look how God used the praisers in 2 Chronicles 20:20-24:

As they set out, [King] Jehoshaphat stood and said, "Listen to me, Judah and people of Jerusalem! Have faith in the LORD your God and you will be upheld; have faith in his prophets and you will be successful."

After consulting the people, Jehoshaphat APPOINTED MEN TO SING TO THE LORD AND TO PRAISE HIM for the splendor of his holiness as they went out at the head of the army, saying: "Give thanks to the LORD, for his love endures forever."

AS THEY BEGAN TO SING AND PRAISE, the LORD set ambushes against the men of Ammon and Moab and Mount Seir who were invading Judah, and they were defeated. The men of Ammon and Moab rose up against the men from Mount Seir to destroy and annihilate them. After they finished slaughtering the men from Seir, they helped to destroy one another.

When the men of Judah came to the place that overlooks the desert and looked toward the vast army, they saw only dead bodies lying on the ground; no one had escaped. [Capitalization mine for emphasis]

That is the awesome power of God at work in response to men's praise of the Lord. The army did not even have to fight because the praisers, who went out in front of the army, won by battling successfully the demons in the spirit realm, and defeating them totally.

Effective prayer is always preceded by prayer. Jesus' disciples saw how Jesus prayed. Effectively! And a strong desire rose up in their hearts and they asked the Lord: Teach us how to pray! Jesus responded,

> ***This, then, is how you should pray: "Our Father in heaven, hallowed be your name, your kingdom come, your will be done on earth as it is in heaven. Give us today our daily bread. Forgive us our debts, as we also have forgiven our debtors. And lead us not into temptation, but deliver us from the evil one."*** [189]

There is an order in prayer! God's order, and the pattern is found in the prayer Jesus taught His disciples. Notice how Jesus began the prayer! He first acknowledged the Sovereignty of God and brought to remembrance who God is! Not for God's sake, but for our sake! We must recognize who God is! Our Father, who lives in heaven, Your name is holy above every name because You are all-holy! Your Kingdom shall come and it shall be established here on earth through Your sons so that Your will can be done here on earth as it is always done in heaven.

Oh, how Sovereign is our God, who rules heaven and earth! ***"The earth is the LORD's, and everything in it, the world, and all who live in it; for he founded it upon the seas and established it upon the waters."*** [190]

God knows who He is! God exists in His Majestic Spirit whether we as men recognize Him or not! Our concept of God

---

[189] Mt. 6:9-13
[190] Ps. 24:1 and 1 Cor. 10:26

does not change His existence, His nature or His essence! Our thoughts about God do not change Him one iota. God is who He says He is. I am who I Am! I am who exists! I am everything that pre-existed My creation which I made from nothing simply by speaking My word! And My Word brought it all forth for My Glory!

Why did Daniel receive such quick responses to his prayers? Because he acknowledged the Sovereignty of God before he made his petitions to God!

> *During the night the mystery was revealed to Daniel in a vision. Then Daniel praised the God of heaven and said, Praise be to the name of God for ever and ever; wisdom and power are his. He changes times and seasons; he sets up kings and deposes them. He gives wisdom to the wise and knowledge to the discerning. He reveals deep and hidden things; he knows what lies in darkness, and light dwells with him. I thank and praise you, O God of my fathers: You have given me wisdom and power, you have made known to me what we asked of you, you have made known to us the dream of the king.*[191]

To acknowledge the Sovereignty of God we must first know who He is! This demands a relationship with Him. And that takes time sitting in His Presence to allow His thoughts to become our thoughts. Jesus and the Father did not have to speak to each other. Why ? Because they thought the same thoughts! The Apostles learned their lesson well from Jesus on how to pray

---

[191] Dan. 2:19-23

effectively!

Look at another example of acknowledging the Sovereignty of God found in Acts 4:23-26:

After they were permitted to go, the Apostles returned to their own company and told all that the chief priests and elders had said to them. And when they heard it, they lifted their voices together with unified mind to God and said, O Sovereign Lord, You are who made the heaven and the earth and the sea, and everything that is in them. Who by the mouth of your forefather, David, Your servant and child, and said through the Holy Spirit, Why did the heathen Gentiles become wanton and insolent and rage, and the people imagine and study and plan vain things—that will not succeed? And the kings of the earth took their stand in array [for attack], and the rulers were assembled and combined against the Lord and against His Anointed, Christ, the Messiah. For in this city they actually met and plotted together against Your holy Child and Servant Jesus, Whom you consecrated by anointing, both Herod and Pontius Pilate with the Gentiles and peoples of Israel to carry out all that Your hand and Your will and purpose had predestined (predetermined) should occur. And, now, Lord, observe their threats and grant Your bond servants [full freedom] to declare Your message fearlessly. While you stretch out Your hand to cure and perform signs and wonders through the authority and by the power of the name of Your holy Child and Servant Jesus. And when they had prayed, the place in which they were assembled was shaken; and they were all filled with the Holy Spirit, and they continued to speak the Word of God with freedom and boldness and courage. [Amplified Bible]

You have no needs when you get into the Sovereignty [Sovereign Will] of God! Acts 4:34,35: *"There were no needy persons among them. For from time to time those who owned lands or houses sold them, brought the money from the sales and put it at the apostles' feet, and it was distributed to anyone as he had need."*

God will supply all your needs: *"But my God shall supply all your need according to his riches in glory by Christ Jesus."* [192]

One day at our prayer group, several messages were delivered; the first was:[193] *You have confessed me with your mouth; you have believed me with your heart, now set thy feet to obedience, and I will stand behind you.* The Lord was saying: Let your prayer be manifested in your daily walk.

Another intercessor spoke about 2 Kgs. 20:1-11, where Hezekiah's powerful prayer for healing and restoration was confirmed by his request for a sign—a miraculous event of making

---

[192] Phil. 4:19 [KJV]

[193] The following men and women were individuals attending our businesspeople's prayer meetings held in my office regularly and afterwards when my office closed, in my home.

"the shadow go back the ten steps it had gone ahead" (actually stopping the earth and reversing its momentum enough to reverse the sun's shadow). God heard it and He moved! God can do anything He chooses! And He does!

Another man read from James 5:17: *"Elijah was a man just like us. He prayed earnestly that it would not rain, and it did not rain on the land for three and a half years. Again he prayed, and the heavens gave rain, and the earth produced its crops."*

A fourth man said we are not to complain or murmur in our difficulties to others who can do nothing about them. Instead, we are to go to God and we won't miss His blessings. Though each of these messages may have had a message for someone else in the room, each had one for me regarding the financial rain that the Lord has promised is coming forth.[194]

God is more interested in the minister than the ministry, so He is preparing our hearts before He sends us forth to do His work! He does not want us to shipwreck on the high seas of the turbulence that is coming to the world system.

After lunch that day a fifth man felt he, as an intercessor,

---

[194] Eccl. 2:26: To the man who pleases him, God gives wisdom, knowledge and happiness, but to the sinner he gives the task of gathering and storing up wealth to hand it over to the one who pleases God. Pr. 13:22: A good man leaves an inheritance for his children's children, but a sinner's wealth is stored up for the righteous.
Mic. 4:12,13: But they do not know the thoughts of the LORD; they do not understand his plan, he who gathers them like sheaves to the threshing floor. 13 "Rise and thresh, O Daughter of Zion, for I will give you horns of iron; I will give you hoofs of bronze and you will break to pieces many nations." You will devote their ill-gotten gains to the LORD, their wealth to the Lord of all the earth.

should pray in agreement with me to claim now the blessings promised: **Set thy feet to obedience.** We praised the Lord and as both of us prayed in tongues, we received various words, such as, **"I am doing a mighty work," "Enlarge your expectations," "Not by might, nor by power, but by My Spirit."** Lord, we claim NOW the blessings you have promised! Praise the Lord! Let it rain NOW, Lord!

One day, March 9, 1992, four intercessors joined me for prayer in the office and there was such a spirit of joy present in spite of our circumstances! Praise God! Someone read from Morris Cerrulo's *5 Major Crises and 5 Major Waves of the Holy Spirit Coming in The 1990's:* "We are to be purified as is gold in the furnace, tried as gold is tried in the fire until all the impurities . . . all the things in our lives which are not of God . . . are burned away. The gold represents the spiritual refining process we are going to experience; we are going to be tried until we come forth as pure gold.

> **But who can endure the day of his coming? Who can stand when he appears? For he will be like a refiner's fire or a launderer's soap. He will sit as a refiner and purifier of silver; he will purify the Levites and refine them like gold and silver. Then the Lord will have men who will bring offerings in righteousness.**[195]

Then I led this prayer: "Lord, only You can purify us with Your power and Your new divine anointing! Give us that new anointing! The same anointing as You promised in Isaiah 42:1: **'I will put my Spirit on him,'** and in Joel 2:28: **'I will pour out**

---

[195] Mal. 3:3

my Spirit on all people. Your sons and daughters will prophesy, your old men will dream dreams, your young men will see visions. Even on my servants, both men and women, I will pour out my Spirit in those days.' Lord Jesus, I pray that everything You have planned to happen in my life will come to pass! Give me a new determination to do Your perfect will, to surrender entirely to You! Praise the Lord!"

CHAPTER 12

Kingdom Economics

Eugene Smith, a pastor from South Africa, was brought to my office by one of the prayer warriors on November 13, 1991. He immediately had a word for me as he entered my office from Hag. 2:6-9:

> *This is what the LORD Almighty says: "In a little while I will once more shake the heavens and the earth, the sea and the dry land. I will shake all nations, and the desired of all nations will come, and I will fill this house with glory," says the LORD Almighty. "The silver is mine and the gold is mine," declares the LORD Almighty. "The glory of this present house will be greater than the glory of the former house," says the LORD Almighty. "And in this place I will grant peace," declares the LORD Almighty.*

This word gave me insight into those Scriptures as they relate to the revival to come upon the earth sovereignly by His Spirit. The Lord intends to release the finances to His Body so they can take His gospel message of the kingdom to the very ends of the earth.

For that very purpose He shall transfer the wealth from the wicked to those righteous people[196] whom He can trust to do His perfect will. Notice that this is kingdom teaching that Jesus taught and preached, not man's teaching. We need to get the

---

[196] Pr. 13:22: The wealth of the sinner [is] laid up for the just.

teaching of this kingdom principle deep into our spirit. Notice the setting for this teaching.

In answer to the disciples' question,

"Why do you speak to the people in parables?" *[Jesus] replied, "THE KNOWLEDGE OF THE SECRETS OF THE KINGDOM OF HEAVEN has been given to you, but not to them. Whoever has will be given more, and he will have an abundance. Whoever does not have, even what he has will be taken from him. This is why I speak to them in parables: 'Though seeing, they do not see; though hearing, they do not hear or understand.'"*[197]

Herein lies the revelation of a kingdom principle for the endtimes. Jesus called it *"the knowledge of the secrets of the kingdom of heaven."* It is regarding the transfer of wealth from the wicked to the righteous for the great endtime harvest of souls.

A paradigm shift is needed in the Church to comprehend what Jesus is saying here. The revelation teaching of Jesus, the Messiah-King, has been distorted. It has been mixed with culture, with history, with pride and with nationalism. But His teaching is pure and unadulterated truth which we must search out. This means we as Christians must alter the pattern of our thinking to that of Jesus' mind. *"The spiritual man makes judgments about all things, but he himself is not subject to any man's judgment: 'For who has known the mind of the Lord that he may instruct him?' But we have the mind*

---

[197] Mt. 13:1-12, 25:29; Lk. 8:18, 19:26 [Capitalization mine for emphasis]

of Christ."[198]

Jesus connects this kingdom teaching with the parable of the sower. The teaching falls directly between the parable of the sower and Jesus' own explanation of that parable.[199]

Jesus is the sower.

The seed is *"the message about the kingdom." "Listen then to what the parable of the sower means: When anyone hears THE MESSAGE ABOUT THE KINGDOM and does not understand it, the evil one comes and snatches away what was sown in his heart."*[200] Demonic forces always are gathering around the people of God to snatch away the message of the kingdom that Jesus sows in the hearts of men.

And the good soil is *"the one who received the seed." "The seed that fell on good soil is the man who hears the word and understands it. He produces a crop, yielding a hundred, sixty or thirty times what was sown."*[201]

Here is what Jesus is saying. Listen with an open mind lest you fall into Jesus' definition of those to whom He chooses to speak in parables. Jesus said: *"This is why I speak to them in parables: 'Though seeing, they do not see; though*

---

[198] 1 Cor. 2:15,16 and Phil. 2:5: Let this mind be in you, which was also in Christ Jesus." [KJV]

[199] Mt. 13:1-12, 25:29; Lk. 8:18, 19:26

[200] Mt. 13:19

[201] Mt. 13:18,19,23 [Capitalization mine for emphasis]

hearing, they do not hear or understand.'''[202]

The worldly, carnal thinking mind cannot **"see"** or **'hear'** this kingdom message! Whether one is an unbeliever or 'an unbelieving believer,' if one eclectically chooses to discard His kingdom message to fit his or her mindset or theology or tradition, that one is likened by Jesus as those who are blind, **"who do not see."**[203] Jesus loves the truth and does not allow an unholy mixture to distort or pervert His kingdom message. In Lev. 10:10 Moses said: **"You must distinguish between the holy and the common, between the unclean and the clean, and you must teach the Israelites all the decrees the LORD has given them through Moses."**[204]

So the spiritual man must distinguish between that which is of God and that which is of man. That spiritual man can then see and hear the kingdom message because he has spiritual eyes to

---

[202] Mt. 13:13

[203] Tit. 1: 13-16: This testimony is true. Therefore, rebuke them sharply, so that they will be sound in the faith 14 and will pay no attention to Jewish myths or to the commands of those who reject the truth. 15 To the pure, all things are pure, but to those who are corrupted and do not believe, nothing is pure. In fact, both their minds and consciences are corrupted. 16 They claim to know God, but by their actions they deny him. They are detestable, disobedient and unfit for doing anything good.

[204] Other Scriptures that warn against diluting this kingdom truth are: Deut. 4:1,2: Hear now, O Israel, the decrees and laws I am about to teach you. Follow them so that you may live and may go in and take possession of the land that the LORD, the God of your fathers, is giving you. 2 Do not add to what I command you and do not subtract from it, but keep the commands of the LORD your God that I give you; Deut. 12:32: See that you do all I command you; do not add to it or take away from it; Rev. 22:18,19: And if anyone takes words away from this book of prophecy, God will take away from him his share in the tree of life and in the holy city, which are described in this book; Pr. 30:5,6: "Every word of God is flawless; he is a shield to those who take refuge in him. 6 Do not add to his words, or he will rebuke you and prove you a liar."

see and ears to hear what the Spirit is saying. He has what one prophet spoke of as **"faith upon his eyes."**[205]

Jesus' kingdom economic system is contrary to the world's economic system controlled by the enemy through greed, manipulation and control. His kingdom economic model is based on love and generous sharing just as in Acts 4:34,35:

> **Neither was there any among them that lacked: for as many as were possessors of lands or houses sold them, and brought the prices of the things that were sold, And laid [them] down at the apostles' feet: and distribution was made unto every man according as he had need.** [KJV]

The world's economic system will fail and fall, because it is controlled by the spirit of mammon, a false god that God has foretold He shall destroy. So we need to look to kingdom teaching to survive. We have been trained to think that we can preach the gospel of Jesus through man-made programs and human effort, relegating ourselves to preaching merely *the gospel of salvation.* However, Jesus wants us to preach the whole, full gospel which He taught—*the gospel of the kingdom.* And in this instance, Jesus teaches that the kingdom paradigm[206] is contrary to the world system.

A prophetic intercessor from Uganda, John Mulinda, spoke at the Israel Convention in Jerusalem in January, 1999, and shared that the Lord had shown him that the cry of intercession in America

---

[205] Taken from a prophetic word given by Elder Dick Gibbons on March 7, 1999.

[206] *Webster's* defines paradigm as setting up an example; a model or a pattern.

presently is not strong enough to overcome the cry of iniquity in the nation. Then he saw Christians in America begin to cry out to God. But it was the wrong cry. God could not answer because it was a cry of fear of losing everything they held dear and not a cry of repentance. Is. 58:1-10 is a clear example of this:

> *"Shout it aloud, do not hold back. Raise your voice like a trumpet. Declare to my people their rebellion and to the house of Jacob their sins. For day after day they seek me out; they seem eager to know my ways, as if they were a nation that does what is right and has not forsaken the commands of its God. They ask me for just decisions and seem eager for God to come near them. 'Why have we fasted,' they say, 'and you have not seen it? Why have we humbled ourselves, and you have not noticed?'*

> *"Yet on the day of your fasting, you do as you please and exploit all your workers. Your fasting ends in quarreling and strife, and in striking each other with wicked fists. You cannot fast as you do today and expect your voice to be heard on high. Is this the kind of fast I have chosen, only a day for a man to humble himself? Is it only for bowing one's head like a reed and for lying on sackcloth and ashes? Is that what you call a fast, a day acceptable to the LORD?*

> *"Is not this the kind of fasting I have chosen: to loose the chains of injustice and untie the cords of the yoke, to set the oppressed free and break*

every yoke? Is it not to share your food with the hungry and to provide the poor wanderer with shelter—when you see the naked, to clothe him, and not to turn away from your own flesh and blood? Then your light will break forth like the dawn, and your healing will quickly appear; then your righteousness will go before you, and the glory of the LORD will be your rear guard. Then you will call, and the LORD will answer; you will cry for help, and he will say: Here am I.

"If you do away with the yoke of oppression, with the pointing finger and malicious talk, and if you spend yourselves in behalf of the hungry and satisfy the needs of the oppressed, then your light will rise in the darkness, and your night will become like the noonday."

In Is. 31:4 the Lord told His chosen people, *"For in that day every one of you will reject the idols of silver and gold your sinful hands have made."*

James 5:1-6 addresses the spirit of mammon:

Now listen, you rich people, weep and wail because of the misery that is coming upon you. Your wealth has rotted, and moths have eaten your clothes. Your gold and silver are corroded. Their corrosion will testify against you and eat your flesh like fire. You have hoarded wealth in the last days. Look! The wages you failed to pay the workmen who mowed your fields are crying out against you. The cries of the harvesters have reached the ears of the Lord Almighty. You have lived on earth in luxury and self-indulgence. You have fattened yourselves in the day of slaughter. You have condemned and murdered innocent men, who were not opposing you.

Jesus is giving us here a paradigm or a model. He is teaching us there is a great difference between **the divine example** [*the kingdom economic system*] and **man's ideas** [*the world economic system*]. It's the world system versus the kingdom model! The world economic system will fall and will be replaced by His kingdom paradigm or kingdom model. Jesus is setting up an example for those believers who truly believe His words and preach His full gospel of the kingdom; after such shall follow great signs and wonders.

Alter the pattern of thought to that of the mind of Jesus and enter into His rest! *"I have told you these things, so that in me you may have peace. In this world you will have trouble. But take heart! I have overcome the world."*[207] Though persecution and suffering will come to all of Jesus' disciples, God will protect His own, those truly sold out to Him and who trust in Him with all their hearts.[208] Paul writes in Phil. 1:14,29,27-30 says:

---

[207] Jn. 16:30

[208] Ps. 12:7: O LORD, you will keep us safe and protect us from such [wicked] people forever. 8 The wicked freely strut about when what is vile is honored among men.
Pr. 3:5-7: Trust in the LORD with all your heart and lean not on your own understanding; 6 in all your ways acknowledge him, and he will make your paths straight. 7 Do not be wise in your own eyes; fear the LORD and shun evil.

Because of my chains, most of the brothers in the Lord have been encouraged to speak the word of God more courageously and fearlessly. . . . I eagerly expect and hope that I will in no way be ashamed, but will have sufficient courage so that now as always Christ will be exalted in my body, whether by life or by death. . . . Whatever happens, conduct yourselves in a manner worthy of the gospel of Christ. Then, whether I come and see you or only hear about you in my absence, I will know that you stand firm in one spirit, contending as one man for the faith of the gospel without being frightened in any way by those who oppose you. This is a sign to them that they will be destroyed, but that you will be saved—and that by God. For it has been granted to you on behalf of Christ not only to believe on him, but also to suffer for him, since you are going through the same struggle you saw I had, and now hear that I still have.

The real question we Christians need to ask ourselves is: **WHY ARE THERE TWO KINGDOMS WITHIN THE CHURCH?**[209] Why has the world influenced the Church instead of the Church influencing the worldly kingdom? The answer is simple. The conflict between the two worlds is within each of us! And only as we are purged of the world within us will the glory of God be made manifest through us with great signs and wonders following![210]

---

[209] Rom. 10:11: As the Scripture says, "Anyone who trusts in him will never be put to shame."

It is only when God has kingdom people believing His kingdom teaching that He will be able to transfer the wealth from the wicked to the righteous. He certainly is not going to transfer the wealth of the wicked in an unholy mixture to Christians who are wicked or unbelieving. It is His desire to transfer the wealth to the righteous because it is the **HARVEST FINANCES NEEDED TO TAKE THE GOSPEL TO THE ENDS OF THE EARTH!** Oh, you unbelieving generation![211]

God will only trust those who trust Him and only those who can hear the Spirit and walk in the Spirit. Otherwise *"the evil one comes and snatches away what was sown in his heart."*

Here in Is. 61:6-9 is the Lord's description of those He can trust to handle His riches, for He owns it all and gives it to whom He chooses:

And you will be called priests of the LORD, you will be named ministers of our God. You will feed

---

[210] Jn. 18:36,37: Jesus said, "My kingdom is not of this world. If it were, my servants would fight to prevent my arrest by the Jews. But now my kingdom is from another place." 37 "You are a king, then!" said Pilate. Jesus answered, "You are right in saying I am a king. In fact, for this reason I was born, and for this I came into the world, to testify to the truth. Everyone on the side of truth listens to me," and Jn. 15:18,19: "If the world hates you, keep in mind that it hated me first. 19 If you belonged to the world, it would love you as its own. As it is, you do not belong to the world, but I have chosen you out of the world. That is why the world hates you.

[211] 2 Cor. 10:3-6: For though we live in the world, we do not wage war as the world does. 4 The weapons we fight with are not the weapons of the world. On the contrary, they have divine power to demolish strongholds. 5 We demolish arguments and every pretension that sets itself up against the knowledge of God, and we take captive every thought to make it obedient to Christ. 6 And we will be ready to punish every act of disobedience, once your obedience is complete.

on the wealth of nations, and in their riches you will boast. Instead of their shame my people will receive a double portion, and instead of disgrace they will rejoice in their inheritance; and so they will inherit a double portion in their land, and everlasting joy will be theirs. 'For I, the LORD, love justice; I hate robbery and iniquity. In my faithfulness I will reward them and make an everlasting covenant with them. Their descendants will be known among the nations and their offspring among the peoples. All who see them will acknowledge that they are a people the LORD has blessed.'

Who are these people? They are tithers who also give generous offerings and alms. They are those who are *"kind to the poor"* and who *"lend to the Lord."* [212] They are those who recognize the *"the wealth of the sinner is laid up for the just."* [213] They are those who will reap what they sow.[214] Yes, *"whoever has will be given more, and he will have an abundance. Whoever does not have, even what he has*

---

[212] Mt. 12:39-41: He answered, "A wicked and adulterous generation asks for a miraculous sign! But none will be given it except the sign of the prophet Jonah. 40 For as Jonah was three days and three nights in the belly of a huge fish, so the Son of Man will be three days and three nights in the heart of the earth. 41 The men of Nineveh will stand up at the judgment with this generation and condemn it; for they repented at the preaching of Jonah, and now one greater than Jonah is here," and Lk. 11:29-31: As the crowds increased, Jesus said, "This is a wicked generation. It asks for a miraculous sign, but none will be given it except the sign of Jonah. 30 For as Jonah was a sign to the Ninevites, so also will the Son of Man be to this generation. 31 The Queen of the South will rise at the judgment with the men of this generation and condemn them; for she came from the ends of the earth to listen to Solomon's wisdom, and now one greater than Solomon is here."

[213] Pr. 19:17

[214] Pr. 13:22

will be taken from him."[215] *"Remember the Lord your God, for it is he who gives you the ability to produce wealth, and so confirms his covenant."*[216] The Lord is looking to and fro for those willing to pay the sacrificial price to confirm His covenant by using the God-given ability which He chooses to give them! For His word says: *"For the eyes of the LORD range throughout the earth to strengthen those whose hearts are fully committed to him."*[217]

On February 7, 1992, I received a word from the Lord: *Did I not say that I would send you the Holy Spirit to lead you? Do not run ahead of the Holy Spirit! Wait upon the Lord for His timing!* I was led to Dan. 12:3: *"Those who are wise will shine like the brightness of the heavens, and those who lead many to righteousness, like the stars for ever and ever."* I was also led to Eccl. 2:26: *"To the man who pleases Him, God gives wisdom, knowledge and happiness, but to the sinner He gives the task of gathering and storing up wealth to hand it over to the one who pleases God."* That's the task of the wicked—to gather and lay up wealth to hand it over to God's chosen ones to fulfill their calling He has given them.

One month earlier on December 30, 1991, the Lord had given me a strong answer to the mental accusations and torment of doubt "the accuser of the brethren"[218] was bringing to my mind regarding the words of the Lord about my calling.

---

[215] Lk. 8:18

[216] Deut. 8:18

[217] 2 Chr. 16:9

[218] In Rev. 12:10 satan, the father of lies is called the accuser of the brethren; also see Job, chapters 1 & 2.

Whatever your calling, guard your heart against those who would snatch away what was sown in your heart by the Lord. This is especially true of those called to preach and teach kingdom principles that Jesus taught. One major protection against this happening is being under proper Scriptural authority. Those not under authority are like wild horses who easily can be led away from their God-given calling. But God sets the solitary in families.[219]

So I prayed and declared it in writing: *In the name of Jesus, satan, I rebuke you! For Scripture says: "The word of the LORD came to me: 'Son of man, what is this proverb you have in the land of Israel: "The days go by and every vision comes to nothing?" Say to them, "This is what the Sovereign LORD says: I am going to put an end to this proverb, and they will no longer quote it in Israel." Say to them, "The days are near when every vision will be fulfilled. For there will be no more false visions or flattering divinations among the people of Israel. But I the LORD will speak what I will, and it shall be fulfilled without delay. For in your days, you rebellious house, I will fulfill whatever I say, declares the Sovereign LORD.""*

"The word of the LORD came to me: 'Son of man, the house of Israel is saying, "The vision he sees is for many years from now, and he prophesies about the distant future." 'Therefore say to them, "This is what the Sovereign LORD says: None of my words will be delayed any longer; whatever I say will be fulfilled, declares the Sovereign LORD."" [220]

---

[219] Ps. 68:6: God setteth the solitary in families: he bringeth out those which are bound with chains: but the rebellious dwell in a dry [land].

"'I will shake all nations, and the desired of all nations will come, and I will fill this house with glory,' says the LORD Almighty. 'The silver is mine and the gold is mine,' declares the LORD Almighty. 'The glory of this present house will be greater than the glory of the former house,' says the LORD Almighty. 'And in this place I will grant peace,' declares the LORD Almighty." [221]

Satan, the Lord is taking back "the silver" and "the gold" that belongs to the Lord which you have falsely claimed too long for your kingdom of evil through greed, avarice and covetousness. God is taking back His stolen property for His Glory, for His Kingdom, by His Spirit in a miraculous way so that all men will know it is His and His doing!

Furthermore, satan, the Lord God has said to me: "You have not chosen Me, but I have chosen you, and have called you to labor in My Harvest vineyard!" [222] *"'On that day,' declares the LORD Almighty, 'I will take you, my servant Zerubbabel son of Shealtiel,' declares the LORD, 'and I will make you like my signet ring, for I have chosen you,' declares the LORD Almighty."* [223] *Begone, satan! Flee forever! Praise God! You are defeated! Jesus has overcome, triumphing over you!* [224]

On December 31, 1991, I wrote: *"We live by faith, not by sight!"* [225] And that is my desire, Lord, that I live and walk

---

[220] Ez. 12:21-28

[221] Hag. 2:7-9

[222] Jn. 15:16

[223] Hag. 2:23

[224] Col. 2:15: And having disarmed the powers and authorities, he made a public spectacle of them, triumphing over them by the cross.

by faith, not by sight, waiting for the Spirit to move! Speak, Lord, that I might hear You! Open my eyes and ears, Lord, that I might see divine realities and hear only the truth!

Oh, satan is so tricky. He has been around a lot longer that we have and he knows human nature very well. He has been studying each of us for generations through our ancestors.

And he knows that the strongest principality to stop God's work on earth is the spirit of anti-christ. Now the word 'christ' means 'anointing' or 'the anointed one.' And we all have an anointing to do the calling of God upon our lives. Those who are called to "spoil the enemy" in the financial realm need to have that special anointing. It will allow them to see and understand the revelation on kingdom economics that those not having such an anointing will never understand. For an explanation of other kinds of anointings see the Introduction to this book.

This special anointing will cause those who do not understand that anointing to even come against those who do! They will operate as the *"accuser of the brethren"*[226] and accuse the anointed ones of manipulating people, stealing from people, of being greedy and even materialistic. That spirit of anti-christ,

---

[225] 2 Cor. 5:7

[226] Rev. 12:10-12: And I heard a loud voice saying in heaven, Now is come salvation, and strength, and the kingdom of our God, and the power of his Christ: for the accuser of our brethren is cast down, which accused them before our God day and night. 11 And they overcame him by the blood of the Lamb, and by the word of their testimony; and they loved not their lives unto the death. 12 Therefore rejoice, [ye] heavens, and ye that dwell in them. Woe to the inhabiters of the earth and of the sea! for the devil is come down unto you, having great wrath, because he knoweth that he hath but a short time. [KJV]

or the spirit of anti-anointing, comes against those anointed to do the will of God they are called to do. If satan can stop the anointing, he can stop the power to remove the yokes and burdens Isaiah spoke of in Is. 10:27: *"And it shall come to pass in that day, [that] his burden shall be taken away from off thy shoulder, and his yoke from off thy neck, and the yoke shall be destroyed because of the anointing."*

But with Christ, the Anointed One, the enemy cannot stop the burden-removing, yoke-destroying power that is in "The Anointing." Gal. 5:1 says: *"Stand fast therefore in the liberty wherewith Christ hath made us free, and be not entangled again with the yoke of bondage."* [KJV]

Remember, Jesus has disarmed the demonic powers and authorities, and He has made a public spectacle of them, triumphing over them by the cross.[227] Jesus "spoiled the enemy" as an example to us! Hallelujah!

"All power in heaven and on earth has been given to Me. Therefore go and make disciples of all nations."[228] We have been given the authority [the right, *exousia* in the Greek] and the power [the might, *dunamis* in the Greek] to rule over the devil. We have the right to use the might to put satan to flight!

---

[227] Col. 2:15: And having disarmed the powers and authorities, he made a public spectacle of them, triumphing over them by the cross.
[228] Mt. 28:18

Blessings or curses—it's our choice![229] Submission to the word of God or rebellion and the devil rules! Is. 1:18-20 tells us that rebellion neutralizes our authority over satan![230] People who constantly mix positives with negatives have zero power! That's a law of mathematics as well as of physics! The same is true in the supernatural realm as it is in the natural.

Be constant in your pursuit! If when someone is up emotionally one minute and down emotionally the next minute, such a one is likened to *"a wave of the sea, blown and tossed by the wind"* as James speaks of in his letter, Jas. 1:2-8:

Consider it pure joy, my brothers, whenever you face trials of many kinds, because you know that the testing of your faith develops perseverance. Perseverance must finish its work so that you may be mature and complete, not lacking any-

---

[229] Deut. 11:26-28: See, I am setting before you today a blessing and a curse-- 27 the blessing if you obey the commands of the LORD your God that I am giving you today; 28 the curse if you disobey the commands of the LORD your God and turn from the way that I command you today by following other gods, which you have not known, and Josh. 24:15-17: But if serving the LORD seems undesirable to you, then choose for yourselves this day whom you will serve, whether the gods your forefathers served beyond the River, or the gods of the Amorites, in whose land you are living. But as for me and my household, we will serve the LORD." 16 Then the people answered, "Far be it from us to forsake the LORD to serve other gods! 17 It was the LORD our God himself who brought us and our fathers up out of Egypt, from that land of slavery, and performed those great signs before our eyes. He protected us on our entire journey and among all the nations through which we traveled.

[230] Is. 1:18-20: "'Come now, let us reason together,' says the LORD. 'Though your sins are like scarlet, they shall be as white as snow; though they are red as crimson, they shall be like wool. 19 If you are willing and obedient, you will eat the best from the land; 20 but if you resist and rebel, you will be devoured by the sword.' For the mouth of the LORD has spoken."

thing. If any of you lacks wisdom, he should ask God, who gives generously to all without finding fault, and it will be given to him. But when he asks, he must believe and not doubt, because he who doubts is like a wave of the sea, blown and tossed by the wind. That man should not think he will receive anything from the Lord; he is a double-minded man, unstable in all he does.

The devil has *dunamis* power but he cannot use it against us unless we open a door to him, thereby giving him the authority to use that power against us. We have *exousia* over the devil's *dunamis*! He has no authority over us unless we come into his territory. If we are enticed through sin into his kingdom, which is his territory, he can mess with us all he wants.

The only time that we can lawfully enter his kingdom of darkness without harm to ourselves or fear of being defeated, is when we come to defeat and conquer him. A repentant heart defeats satan, for he fears and flees from a repentant heart! In fact, he cannot understand repentance! That is a foreign concept to him and it scrambles his brains and drives him insane to even be near a repentant heart! He has no authority and no power over a repentant sinner because that sinner is called an overcomer by Jesus![231]

Even if persecution comes against us, consider such as pure joy:

---

[231] Rev. 2:26,27: To him who overcomes and does my will to the end, I will give authority over the nations-- 27 'He will rule them with an iron scepter; he will dash them to pieces like pottery'-- just as I have received authority from my Father.

Do not be afraid of what you are about to suffer. I tell you, the devil will put some of you in prison to test you, and you will suffer persecution for ten days. Be faithful, even to the point of death, and I will give you the crown of life. He who has an ear, let him hear what the Spirit says to the churches. He who overcomes will not be hurt at all by the second death.[232] *The kingdom of God is not a matter of talk but of power.*[233]

On Saturday, February 15, 1992, I spent a couple of hours reading the Scriptures and praying. At about 12:30 AM on Sunday, the Lord impressed upon me to re-read the sections of Ps. 20:2,4,7,9 that had been spoken over me on January 9, 1991. As I read it, the Lord said,

I will do everything therein prayed for: I will "send you help from the sanctuary and grant you support from Zion. . . . And give you the desire of your heart and make all your plans succeed. . . . Some trust in chariots and some in horses, but we trust in the name of the LORD our God. . . . O LORD, save the king! Answer us when we call!"

Praise the Lord!

On Friday morning, April 10, 1992, I had breakfast with Jim Partington. Afterwards we prayed for each other; then Jim had a prophecy for me:

---

[232] Rev. 2:10,11
[233] 1 Cor. 4:20

The Lord thy God shall put a wall of protection around thee; He shall put a wall of fire around thee. He shall be thy glory and transport thee atop the wall without any human effort on thy part. He shall increase thy vision, and give thee a different, greater vision than thou hast before. Thou shall know the Mighty God is alive in thee and working in thy life.

After I arrived at the office and shared this, one of my intercessors said that this prophecy reminded him of Zech. 2:5: *"'And I myself will be a wall of fire around it [Jerusalem],' declares the Lord, 'and I will be its glory within.'"* Praise God!

At this time, the Lord was telling me that He will use our companies in a mighty way so that the whole world will know that these are His companies, His instruments to control what is His:

"I will shake all nations, and the desired of all nations will come, and I will fill this house with glory," says the LORD Almighty. "The silver is mine and the gold is mine," declares the Lord Almighty. "The glory of this present house will be greater than the glory of the former house," says the Lord Almighty.[234]

---

[234] Notice in Hag. 2:7-9 how the Lord sandwiches "the silver" and "the gold" which He says is "Mine" in between two sentences that declare His Glory of this present house! His endtime plan of transferring the wealth to the righteous for the great harvest is clearly stated here for those who have ears to hear what the Spirit is saying to the Church today. It is time that everything which belongs to God be used for His glory and His will--salvation harvest for all who will receive Him as Lord and Savior!

But remember, the Lord says: *"I am among you as one who serves."*[235] He wants us to be distribution centers for others. Lord, give me obedience and humility! And protect me from those offering false wisdom and *"having a form of godliness, but denying the power thereof."*[236]

At the Friday noon prayer meeting on April 10th, while praying, I saw a vision of *many restaurants in a row and the Lord gave me the words: If you come to the right one, I will give you a free meal.* Jesus will freely feed those who are His! The Lord owns it all! Ps. 47:2 exclaims: *"How awesome is the LORD Most High, the great King over all the earth!"* Ps. 24:1 says: *"The earth is the LORD's, and everything in it, the world, and all who live in it."*

On Holy Saturday, April 18, 1992, I went to a restaurant before we went to visit my mother. While there, I was ministered to by the Lord through Psalm 2, especially 2:8: *"Ask of me, and I will make the nations your inheritance, the ends of the earth your possession." The Lord said that though this Psalm was prophetically spoken of His Divine Son, it was also applicable to what He is about to do with us through our company and ministry. As president of the company, I will be perceived by "the kings of the earth" and "the rulers" who "gather together against the Lord and His Anointed One" to have the royalty, dignity and authority promised by the Lord: "'I have installed my King on Zion, my holy hill.'"* (Ps. 2:2-6,8) I am humbled in awe of His Majesty!

---

235 Lk. 22:29

236 2 Tim. 3:5

Jesus said He is King of kings! We are all called to be kings under the King![237] It is time we stop putting up with false humility and strange doctrines, and start recognizing the truth— we are kings! Hallelujah! He uses whom He chooses!

Look at the word of God in this regard. Here is another kingdom paradigm shift needed in our thinking.

They [the worldly kings who have sold out to the devil] will make war against the Lamb, but the Lamb will overcome them because he is Lord of lords and King of kings—and with him will be his called, chosen and faithful followers.[238] On his robe and on his thigh he has this name written: KING OF KINGS AND LORD OF LORDS.[239] Grace and peace to you from him who is, and who was, and who is to come, and from the seven spirits before his throne, and from Jesus Christ, who is the faithful witness, the firstborn from the dead, and THE RULER OF THE KINGS of the earth. To him who loves us and has freed us from our sins by his blood, AND HAS MADE US TO BE A KINGDOM AND PRIESTS to serve his God and Father— to him be glory and power for ever and ever! Amen.[240] If we endure, we will also reign with

---

237 Rev. 1:6: And hath made us kings and priests unto God and his Father; to him [be] glory and dominion for ever and ever. Amen. [KJV]

238 Rev. 17:14

239 Rev. 19:16

240 Rev. 1:4-6 [Capitalization mine for emphasis]

241 2 Tim. 2:12

him.[241] ***Blessed and holy are those who have part in the first resurrection. The second death has no power over them, but they will be priests of God and of Christ and will reign with him for a thousand years.***[242]

Our company has a mission to the world! I couldn't help but think that this is a fulfillment of His word given me from Is. 48:6-7: ***"From now on I will tell you of new things, of hidden things unknown to you. They are created now, and not long ago; you have not heard of them before today."*** This also is a confirmation of Jim Partington's prophecy of April 10th, 1992. Praise God!

On April 20th, while reading Scripture, the Lord spoke a rhema word concerning **royalty that will be yours,** as spoken on December 7, 1991, and confirmed it with Rom. 11:29: ***"God's gifts and his call are irrevocable."*** Then, I met with one of the intercessors and shared the royalty rhema with him. He shared with me that he felt today was a day of new beginnings and that he should be spending time here in my office, awaiting the Lord's direction for himself. In our discussion, he cited two Scripture passages for my thoughts: Pr. 19:6: ***"Many curry favor with a ruler, and everyone is the friend of a man who gives gifts,"*** and Pr. 29:26: ***"Many seek an audience with a ruler, but it is from the Lord that man gets justice."*** He cautioned that I be discerning regarding people who would want to "latch on" to me because of my calling, much like Simon the sorcerer who envied the gift of laying on of hands by the apostles.[243]

---

242 Rev. 20:6

On Tuesday, April 21, 1992, one intercessor phoned to tell me that the Lord told her the Lord was about to bestow on me the Gift of Faith. This is not to be confused with the faith that bestows salvation, or the faith that grows by reading the Word or by prayer. **THIS IS THE GIFT THAT COMMANDS THE MIRACULOUS TO HAPPEN THROUGH THE POWER OF JESUS! BUT NO DOUBT IS EVER PERMITTED! NEVER! NO DOUBT EVER! AND THE MIRACULOUS WILL HAPPEN!**[244] Praise God! This is exactly the kind of faith that is needed to call forth those things that are not and they become, just as our father Abraham did![245]

---

[243] Acts 8:18-23: When Simon saw that the Spirit was given at the laying on of the apostles' hands, he offered them money 19 and said, "Give me also this ability so that everyone on whom I lay my hands may receive the Holy Spirit." 20 Peter answered: "May your money perish with you, because you thought you could buy the gift of God with money! 21 You have no part or share in this ministry, because your heart is not right before God. 22 Repent of this wickedness and pray to the Lord. Perhaps he will forgive you for having such a thought in your heart. 23 For I see that you are full of bitterness and captive to sin."

[244] This is one of the nine major gifts of the Holy Spirit spoken of in 1 Cor. 12:7-11: Now to each one the manifestation of the Spirit is given for the common good. 8 To one there is given through the Spirit the message of **wisdom**, to another the message of **knowledge** by means of the same Spirit, 9 to another **faith** by the same Spirit, to another gifts of **healing** by that one Spirit, 10 to another **miraculous powers**, to another **prophecy**, to another **distinguishing between spirits,** to another speaking in different kinds of **tongues,** and to still another the **interpretation of tongues.** 11 All these are the work of one and the same Spirit, and he gives them to each one, just as he determines. [Italics mine] They are often times divided into three major groupings: **The Word [or Utterance] Gifts:** Tongues, Interpretation of Tongues and Prophecy; **The Revelation Gifts:** Wisdom, Knowledge and Discernment of Spirits; and **The Power Gifts**: Faith, Healing and Miracles.

[245] Rom. 45:16,17: Therefore, the promise comes by faith, so that it may be by grace and may be guaranteed to all Abraham's offspring--not only to those who are of the law but also to those who are of the faith of Abraham. He is the father of us all. 17 As it is written: "I have made you a father of many nations." He is our father in the sight of God, in whom he believed--the God who gives life to the dead and calls things that are not as though they were.

On Wednesday morning, April 22, 1992, I went to a restaurant to spend quiet time, and while there, Is. 60, 61 and 62 ministered to me:

The glory of the Lord rises upon you. . . . The Lord rises upon you and his glory appears over you. Nations will come to your light, and kings to the brightness of your dawn. Lift up your eyes and look about you: All assemble and come to you; your sons come from afar, and your daughters are carried on the arm. Then you will look and be radiant, your heart will throb and swell with joy; the wealth on the seas will be brought to you, to you the riches of the nations will come. Herds of camels will cover your land, young camels of Midian and Ephah. And all from Sheba will come, bearing gold and incense and proclaiming the praise of the Lord. . . . The Spirit of the Sovereign Lord is on me, because the Lord has anointed me to preach good news to the poor. He has sent me to bind up the brokenhearted, to proclaim freedom for the captives and release from darkness for the prisoners. . . . The nations will see your righteousness, and all kings your glory; you will be called by a new name that the mouth of the Lord will bestow. You will be a crown of splendor in the Lord's hand, a royal diadem in the hand of your God.[246]

Indeed, in order to accomplish God's will on earth, we need this gift of faith to call forth those things that be not and they

---

[246] Is. 60:1-6; 61:1; 62:2,3

become reality! And God gets all the glory! Praise the Lord!

On Monday morning, April 13th, the Lord impressed upon me to read Psalms 93, 95 and 96 and Isaiah 2:1-22. Each stressed God's Majesty and what He is about to do in His own time, drawing men to Him: ***"Splendor and majesty are before him . . . the mountains melt like wax before the Lord . . . the mountain of the Lord's temple will be established as chief among the mountains; it will be raised above the hills, and all nations will stream to it."*** OH, THE SPLENDOR OF HIS MAJESTY!

An intercessor phoned and said she had prayed some time for protection against danger and for protection against well-meaning Christians who would interfere with the Lord's work. Thinking they are doing a good thing, those not walking in the Spirit but in the flesh might pray carnal, witchcraft prayer. I thanked her. Praise the Lord.

Any Christian praying his or her own will instead of God's will, is praying witchcraft prayer which is contrary to the will of God. Any prayer that attempts to control a situation is contrary to His will. Some Christians do not know the difference between praying the will of God and praying their own will to be done on earth. ***"Thy kingdom come. Thy will be done in earth, as [it is] in heaven."***[247]

On Holy Thursday, April 16th, in the morning, the Lord spoke powerfully to me as I was reading in Isaiah 46:9-10: **"I am God, and there is no other; I am God, and there is none like me. . . . I say: My purpose will stand, and I**

---

[247] Mt. 6:10

will do all that I please. . . . What I have said, that will I bring about; what I have planned, that will I do." And Is. 48:6-7: **"From now on I will tell you of new things, of hidden things unknown to you. They are created now, and not long ago; you have not heard of them before today."** Later when I read this to one dear brother, he said years ago he was given Jer. 33:3 for his business: **"Call to me and I will answer you and tell you great and unsearchable things you do not know."**

The Lord is looking for those He can trust to manage His wealth on this earth to bring in His great endtime harvest! The Lord is so good to His faithful people.

CHAPTER 13

Revival is on its Way—Sovereignly

On December 28, 1991, I awoke suddenly with a dramatic and extraordinarily vivid dream-vision which the Lord gave me. This had never happened to me before. I immediately asked the Lord for three confirmations to prove to me without any doubt that this was truly from Him. I received all three confirmations I had asked for, and wrote them down describing each in every detail.

However, the full dream-vision will have to wait for the public to know until such time as the Lord permits me to share it beyond my innermost circle of prayer warriors.[248] I will only say that the dream-vision had to do with dramatic events related to revival that will upset the status quo of our civilization and lead to a Sovereign Move of God upon the earth. It was depicted by tremendous, major forces of nature that I will simply call: The Force Majeure.[249]

I saw thousands upon thousands coming into the kingdom,

---

[248] Several faithful business people for many years met with me in my office on a weekly basis to pray that our companies' destinies as predestined by the Lord would come forth to build His Kingdom here on earth.

[249] My full testimony of what the Lord has been doing in my life up to the present time will have to wait for such a time as the Lord allows me to share everything with the public that He has called me to do. For now, dear reader, you just will have to be satisfied with the prophecies and journaling the Lord permits me to share. The Lord willing, my complete story, *THE TESTIMONY OF JESUS: THE SPIRIT OF PROPHECY as spoken to one of His servant scribes - Books 2, 3, 4* shall most likely come out in a series of books as a follow-up of this first, *Book 1*, at some future date. You certainly can join us in prayer that God's Kingdom come and that God's will be done, on earth as it is in heaven.

and I knew I had seen a vision of the harvest. The following is the way I described it on the morning immediately after the vision: *"A great repentance and revival began, as fear fell over the land; and the national and international media and curiosity seekers as well as believers started flocking out to see the majestic work of God. Not all who came repented, but none dared ridicule."*

Of the many books I read after this time, one book especially confirmed much of what I had been shown and impacted me greatly. It was Rick Joyner's *The Harvest*. The message is one of revival which is so relevant today, ten years after it was written. My heart was burning within me while I read that book.

Lord, send us revival! Send Your Spirit to sovereignly move upon us and lead us to true repentance! Lord, You will do this even without our approval or consent because You are a Sovereign God and You will get all the glory! Your will be done, not ours! No one can manipulate or plan what is only a move of Your Spirit!

Holiness, Truth and The Presence of God, written by Francis Frangipane, had attracted much of my time during this season as well, giving me a greater hunger for seeking the Lord Himself rather than His gifts. *"Blessed are those who hunger and thirst for righteousness, for they will be filled."* [250]

This hunger for righteousness will attract true revival. For the Lord said,

---

[250] Mt. 5:6

When I shut up the heavens so that there is no rain, or command locusts to devour the land or send a plague among my people, if my people, who are called by my name, will humble themselves and pray and seek my face and turn from their wicked ways, then will I hear from heaven and will forgive their sin and will heal their land." [251]

When this seeking His face and turning from our wicked ways happens, there will be no need to look for the harvest because the harvest will be looking for us, His *"people."*

Gösta Öman, who has experienced the breaking forth of revival in several countries in the world, defines revival as "praying, praying, praying without giving up—praying for the Lord to come into a repentant heart. It is prejudgment on a sinner to save him rather than condemn him." [252] Revival is nothing more than returning to God and living the way we should have been living all along. Do not think that all difficulties are the result of satan's work. God disciplines those whom He loves! He wants us to live in His peace and joy on this earth. Is. 26:12 says: *"LORD, you establish peace for us; all that we have accomplished you have done for us."*

The testimony of Isaiah 26:12 was that of the Israelites in the desert, described in Ex. 9:19; 13:20,21, and should be ours as well:

Because of your great compassion you did not

---

[251] 2 Chron. 7:13,14

[252] Gösta Öman is the author of *The Rice Miracle*, also available through Gold Spirit Ministries, Inc.

abandon them in the desert. By day the pillar of cloud did not cease to guide them on their path, nor the pillar of fire by night to shine on the way they were to take. . . . By day the LORD went ahead of them in a pillar of cloud to guide them on their way and by night in a pillar of fire to give them light, so that they could travel by day or night. Neither the pillar of cloud by day nor the pillar of fire by night left its place in front of the people.

I prayed: "Lord, *'we will shout for joy when you are victorious and will lift up our banners in the name of our God. May the LORD grant all your requests. Now I know that the LORD saves his anointed; he answers him from his holy heaven with the saving power of his right hand.'"*[253]

My heart's desire is to see the great endtime harvest come forth in my day! Come, Holy Spirit—move sovereignly!

---

[253] Ps. 20:5,6

CHAPTER 14

God Speaks Loudly with Love in the Woodshed![254]

On February 25, 1992, I was frustrated with the delay of things coming to pass in my life, so on my way to work I said aloud: Lord, You have to speak to me, and You have to speak to me today!

Two brothers joined me in prayer and one prophesied over me:

I speak to you in many ways. And I have spoken My word to you whenever you have tested Me; and I have answered your every prayer through My word, through My prophets, through My anointing on you and through My quiet whisperings. Still you have fears and doubts that it is I who am working mightily through you. What more can I do that I have not done? I cannot give you any more than I have because you do not respond when I beckon you. Hear Me when I speak and follow My instructions. Come to Me with your fears and doubts, and do not go to other men who can do nothing without Me. [A powerful

---

[254]There is a proverbial expression for being corrected by discipline: I was taken to the woodshed. The woodshed is the place where the 'paddle of persuasion' or spanking took place. Even Paul in Heb. 12: 5-7 refers to discipline as a word of encouragement: And ye have forgotten the exhortation which speaketh unto you as unto children, My son, despise not thou the chastening of the Lord, nor faint when thou art rebuked of him: 6 For whom the Lord loveth he chasteneth, and scourgeth every son whom he receiveth. 7 If ye endure chastening, God dealeth with you as with sons; for what son is he whom the father chasteneth not? [KJV]

anointing fell on both of us.[255]]

When you feel My anointing, know that you are to pray with those around you; if you are alone, know that I either want you to pray for someone specifically that I give you, or I am speaking to you directly. Be still and be quiet and know that I want to speak to you! Listen! And obey! I have so much for you to do and it is "by My Spirit!" Abandon your human faith for a walk of faith in My Spirit. Walk in My Spirit and leave behind the things of the flesh so you can desire to possess the things of the Spirit. For if you desire things of the world, that is all you will ever have is worldly things that will pass away. I love you with an unconditional love, and even if you would never respond to My love, I still love you and all men unconditionally. I want you to love with a similar unconditional love. Stop questioning Me; hear My word and see My love!

I responded in prayer,

O Lord, I thank You for speaking to me so boldly. I thank You for the scolding I deserved for doubting Your words and Your prophetic utterances, and for not listening in quiet when Your anointing falls on me as it does so very often, and for not sharing my fears and doubts with You rather than men. Lord, I repent! Lord, I feel purged and cleansed as Isaiah felt after You touched his mouth with the burning

---

[255] This anointing was like the presence of God upon me, which is different than the anointing to spoil.

coal. Thank You for Your unconditional love for me! Lord, I thank You for this close encounter with You! Lord, continue to speak to me and I will listen in quiet to Your still small voice. Lord, open my spiritual ears to hear Your voice; I will respond generously and with a spirit of faith when You beckon me. I love You and I praise You, Lord. Thank You, Jesus! What a purging and loving walk to the woodshed![256]

During the several days after this experience, the anointing fell on me so frequently that I was filled with a special joy[257] that I had never experienced before.

On Friday, February 28, 1992, as I opened a book I intended to read, I found a copy of a typed prophecy that was spoken on July 17th and 18th, 1990, to the Body of Christ. It was spoken through a lady after sitting under the anointed ministry of Morris Cerullo's World Evangelism on video, *The New Anointing*. But this day the Lord dynamically spoke to my heart through that word of prophecy as if it was delivered afresh to me.

I share this because many times words spoken to an individual are meant for others who are open to receive the Lord's word. If a prophetic word spoken to another seems to apply directly to you and ministers to you, claim it for yourself. I know a pastor who is like a vacuum cleaner; he just sucks up everything

---

256 Heb. 12:9,10: Moreover, we have all had human fathers who disciplined us and we respected them for it. How much more should we submit to the Father of our spirits and live! Our fathers disciplined us for a little while as they thought best; but God disciplines us for our good, that we may share in his holiness.

257 Gal 5:22,23: But the fruit of the Spirit is love, joy, peace, longsuffering, gentleness, goodness, faith, 23 Meekness, temperance: against such there is no law. [KJV]

anyone else doesn't claim for themselves. He says, "I get all I can, and I can all I get," implying he stores it away for future need and use. This does not imply that any or every prophecy one might like is applicable to a person. But if that person feels drawn at the Lord's leading toward that prophetic word, that word could well apply to more than just the one over which the prophecy is spoken. Spiritual discernment and pastoral guidance is needed in this area.

Here is the word of the lady:

This thing that you have desired of Me, I have given it to you. Just walk in it yielded to My Spirit. I am fulfilling My Purpose, Plan and Design by My Spirit. Don't be afraid. Fear not, for I love you. I am your God and the Shepherd of My fold. I will lead you into this way and manifestation of My power. Walk in it without hesitation or human effort or wisdom. Walk by My Spirit, not by human intellect or power. I am doing it through you by My Spirit. Just let My Spirit flow through you. Just trust and obey Me! Do not be anxious for anything.

Don't try to make it happen. Just rest in Me, in My Timing, My Plan and My Purpose. The work is finished. Rest in Me! Enter into My Rest and My Creative Power! Many distractions will come along, but stay right here in My Presence, basking in it. My Purpose, My Plan, My Design for your life is going forth. It is proceeding as planned. I love you and everything that I promised you will come to pass. Just continue to trust Me and to praise Me, and see it unfold right before your eyes. And within your being will flow the rivers of Living Water. And Power from on high will envelope you, will overtake you, will cause you to be all that I designed you to be from the foundation of the world. Nothing can stop it now. It is truly finished. The seeds were sown, the soil was prepared, the ground was tilled and cultivated. The tears watered it. My Light and Countenance shined upon it. My Spirit directed and My Power caused it to spring forth and bear fruit.

Now it is harvest time. I am the Lord of the Harvest. I will show you how to bring in the sheaves by My Spirit and My Power, says the Lord of Hosts. The only tools needed are your obedience, praise and thanksgiving. I have imparted the Supernatural Faith, MY FAITH, the Faith of God which is activated as you praise Me and agree with My Words which are self-fulfilling.

I responded: Lord, I hear You loudly and clearly! I hear Your voice and I will obey You! Praise the Lord! Ps. 33:11 came to mind: *"But the plans of the Lord stand firm forever, the purposes of His heart through all generations!"* What a loving God we serve! I pray that all others You are calling, especially those called to help me fulfill Your vision and ministry for my life, would hear and obey Your voice as well! Praise God! Ps. 34:4: *"I sought the Lord, and He answered me; He delivered me from all my fears."*

173

On Saturday, February 29, 1992, the Lord Jesus revealed to me: *If you only believe Me in your head but fail to experience My power in your life, you don't really know Me as Jesus, the Son of God.*[258] *These signs and wonders will follow believers! Get ready for My power to manifest in your life!*

Let my prayer, Lord, be like Paul's words which he wrote in 1 Cor. 1:18, 2:4,5 and Phil. 3:10-14:

For the message of the cross is foolishness to those who are perishing, but to us who are being saved it is the power of God. . . . My message and my preaching were not with wise and persuasive words, but with a demonstration of the Spirit's power, so that your faith might not rest on men's wisdom, but on God's power. . . . I want to know Christ and the power of his resurrection and the fellowship of sharing in his sufferings, becoming like him in his death, and so, somehow, to attain to the resurrection from the dead. Not that I have already obtained all this, or have already been made perfect, but I press on to take hold of that for which Christ Jesus took hold of me. Brothers, I do not consider myself yet to have taken hold of it. But one thing I do: Forgetting what is behind and straining toward what is ahead, I press on toward the goal to win the prize for which God has called me heavenward in Christ Jesus.

---

258 Mk. 16:17,18: And these signs shall follow them that believe; In my name shall they cast out devils; they shall speak with new tongues; 18 They shall take up serpents; and if they drink any deadly thing, it shall not hurt them; they shall lay hands on the sick, and they shall recover.

Trips to the woodshed would become much more unnecessary if we all would learn the meaning of this phrase: Seek His face, and not His hands! It focuses our attention of the Creator rather than the things of creation. *"But seek first his kingdom and his righteousness, and all these things will be given to you as well. Therefore do not worry about tomorrow, for tomorrow will worry about itself. Each day has enough trouble of its own."* [259]

On Tuesday, March 3, 1992, as soon as I woke up, I said to my wife, "Today is the day the Lord has made! Praise God!" My spirit was filled with joy and anticipation of what the Lord would do today! *"For the kingdom of God is not a matter of talk but of power."* [260]

After attending a prayer breakfast, I went to the office to write my testimony and to journal. The Lord led me to this Scripture: *"But remember the Lord your God, for it is he who gives you the ability to produce wealth, and so confirms his covenant, which he swore to your forefathers, as it is today."* [261]

I responded: I praise You, Lord! What a mighty and loving God we serve! Praise Him all you creatures!

Praise God in his sanctuary; praise him in his mighty heavens. Praise him for his acts of power; praise him for his surpassing greatness. [262] *I will*

---

[259] Mt. 6:33
[260] 1 Cor. 4:20
[261] Deut. 8:18
[262] Ps. 150:1,2

exalt you, my God the King; I will praise your name for ever and ever . . . You open your hand and satisfy the desires of every living thing.[263]

Praise you, Lord!

---

[263] Ps. 145:16

CHAPTER 15

Let Us Fix Our Eyes on Jesus

Spiritual people move from one level to another higher level as they come closer to Jesus and enter into a deeper relationship with Him. The following is recounted to show the reader at what level our prayer group was during this time.

On the afternoon of March 9, 1992, UPS delivered a package to me from Pagosa Springs, Colorado. Peter Laue sent a most beautiful plaque: **LET US FIX OUR EYES ON JESUS** (Heb.12:2) in gold letters. Praise God! Also a note dated 3/4/92 from Peter:

Dear Laverne,

When light reflects from the letters on your sign it is hard to ignore the sign. I pray that the words will drive out all darkness and convict sinners of their sins. I say that because it is easy for an imposter to infiltrate our ranks if our own hearts are not pure. Satan is the master deceiver. But there must be a reason why Jesus permitted a "Judas" in His group of disciples. We had an imposter in our house for almost 4 weeks. When he revealed his true nature last Friday, it was as if I was looking Satan straight in the face. We have learned much through this situation. When we talk the next time I will share some of the insights that were revealed to us. God has everything under control and He loves you.

Much love,
Peter and Rebekah

A small card was attached to the wood plague which pro-claimed: FREEDOM TO THE CAPTIVES THROUGH [OUR CORPORATE NAME] INC.!

At our prayer meeting one brother asked that I read Ps. 76 about the power of God when we worship Him. We had Peter and Rebekah Laue from Pagosa Springs join us for prayer by phone. Peter requested prayer for the fear he had recently experienced and woke up with the morning after a restless night.

I prayed for Peter in the name of Jesus that all power of fear over him would be destroyed now, that he would be filled with wis-dom, revelation knowledge, spiritual understanding and divine discernment. Another brother suggested we pray Psalm 54:2-17 over Peter:

> *'Enlarge the place of your tent. . . . Do not be afraid; you will not suffer shame . . . the Lord will call you . . . though the mountains be shaken . . . my unfailing love for you will not be shaken nor my covenant of peace be removed . . . I will build you . . . I will make your battlements . . . in right-eousness you will be established . . . terror will be far removed . . . no weapon forged against you will prevail, and you will refute every tongue that accuses you. This is the heritage of the servants of the Lord, and this is their vindication from me,' declares the Lord.*

This brother also advised Peter and Rebekah to walk the boundaries of their property, claiming them for the Lord alone. Protection is yours when it belongs to the Lord. The devil may have possession of your property because he is a thief and robber, but he does not have the title! We need to claim it back![264] ***"The earth is the Lord's and everything in it!"*** [265] Evict the devil from God's premises!

Another brother prayed and proclaimed victory for Peter. Peter then prayed for a member of our group so that he would not be anxious, but rest in the Lord, and let Him be glorified by doing His work His way; that he would fully realize he is a vehicle in God's hands for His Glory; that someone with whom he is negotiating needs to surrender his will to God's plan. Also, that any imposter that might be in his camp would be exposed now. And that the Lord would keep out anyone who would not be harmonious with the Lord's plan and transactions; that he would find peace in his life, power and direction from the Lord against great odds, bringing great victory and glory to God.

Peter then spoke to me and said, "Keep the presence of God in your life. It is so easy to know that we are undertaking a task for God that we forget to have the presence of God. In Catherine Marshall's book she says, 'Do not forfeit the presence of God.'" ***"Let us fix our eyes on Jesus."*** [266]

Then Peter prayed for me and three others about to make a business trip: "Father God, I pray for the trip to California. Lord, I'm filled with joy! I pray for a rich blessing. I pray for this pilgrimage to a place you have established. I pray for their faith,

---

264 Joel 2:25: 25 And I will restore to you the years that the locust hath eaten, the cankerworm, and the caterpiller, and the palmerworm, my great army which I sent among you.

265 Ps. 24:1 and 1 Cor. 10:26

266 Heb.12:2

obedience and commitment that will be tested. Father God, I pray you will have your way. I pray they will leave everything at home that they do not need. I pray for those who are anxious; turn that anxiety into anticipation. Sometimes, Father God, you work quickly. *'With the Lord a day is like a thousand years and a thousand years are like a day.'*[267] I pray their hearts will be so pure that they will discover your riches. I pray this to be a trip of revelation, unity among all who go. Pour out your Spirit upon them[268] that they will be seen as your representatives in restaurants, gas stations and motels. I pray that they receive healing—emotional, spiritual or physical. Protect them. You have made a large investment in these people. I pray what you have raised up will not be stolen. Father God, rebuke the imposter, the Judas, if there be one! Father God, I pray new exploits in the name of Jesus! Just be aggressive! Praise God!"

I recount these prayers in our sessions to give the reader an idea of what level of intercession we were at in this point of our lives.

CHAPTER 16

The Anointing

Over the weekend of March 15ᵗʰ, 1992, I spent many hours reading Benny Hinn's book *The Anointing!* What a blessing! This was my first serious introduction to Benny Hinn. The Lord told me that what He taught me, I am to show others, for the same is meant for them: *"Preach the Word; be prepared in season and out of season; correct, rebuke and encourage—with great patience and careful instruction,"*[269] Though I did not intend to share these things with others, the Lord had other plans: *"A man's steps are directed [ordered in The Amplified] by the Lord."*[270] Praise the Lord!

The presence of God, and the subsequent power of God He is giving me, are meant for all that seriously desire His Truth and His Gifts. I am not unique as some might suggest, for He has called many. For though *"many are called, few will be chosen"* by Him, because He says that *"in the last days . . . men shall be lovers of their own selves, . . . proud, . . . having a form of godliness, but denying the power thereof; . . . ever learning, and never able to come to the knowledge of the truth."*[271][KJV] It is not enough to hear the word of God, but to be a doer of the word as well.[272] Jas. 1:22 says, *"Do not merely listen to the word, and so deceive yourselves. Do what it says."* He is looking for a few faithful

---

269 2 Tim. 4:2

270 Pr. 20:24

271 1 Tim. 3:1-7

272 Lk. 11:28: He replied, "Blessed rather are those who hear the word of God and obey it."

people, who will be faithful and persevere to the very end! When the Lord calls, we must answer.

We must seek Jesus, who is **"the Way, the Truth and the Life."** [273] Jesus wants all of us to know the Presence of God and the Power of God! Holy Spirit, help me receive everything You have to give me to serve You; I want Your Anointing! And, Holy Spirit, help me to tell others that *the Anointing is for every Christian who desires the fullness of God.*

In fact, the Lord showed me that this book is not to be simply my testimony as much as a *HOW TO MANIFEST GOD'S GLORY INSTRUCTION BOOK* so others can learn to do the same. More of a Manual than a Testimony! Praise God! Many desire to experience God's power in their life, but really don't know how to make it happen.[274]

Dear reader, if you are a serious follower of Jesus, let this be your daily prayer: God, give me the anointing of Your Holy Spirit, now and every day. Remove all dross (iniquity) from my life so I shall be able, through Your Grace, to receive this anointing! Thank you, Lord! **"He must increase that I might decrease!"** [275]

Once, at an earlier meeting of The School of the Holy Spirit held by Burton Seavey, he commented, "Some people ask me: 'What do I need to do to get the anointing?' Like draws like! Hey, the first thing I know what to do if I want the anointing, is hang around people who have it! That's not the only thing, but

[273] Jn. 14:6

[274] The best practical book I have found that explains getting in God's glory is Ruth Ward Heflin's books, **Glory: Experiencing the Atmosphere of Heaven, Revival Glory** and **River Glory**.

[275] Jn. 3:30

that's a sure-fire way to start you toward it! Hang around people who have got it! It'll make you hungry for it! Hallelujah! Hallelujah!"

The Lord speaks to me daily through the Word, prayer, spiritual reading, my fellowship with Christian brothers and sisters, circumstances and through the anointing that falls. All of these are daily events! Praise God! Each of us need to just open our eyes to what the Spirit wants to show us daily!

The best explanation of the anointing, which I had begun to experience so strongly at this time in my life, I found in Benny Hinn's book, *The Anointing.* Everything in his book was a confirmation of what the Lord has taught me, and I believe that by prayerfully reading his book, along with your daily Scripture reading, the Lord will show you how you can experience the Presence and the Power of God in an understandable and achievable way. Praise God! That is my prayer for you.

That Friday evening, March 20th, some family and friends joined me at The Chicago Pavilion to hear Benny Hinn minister. What a mighty God we serve! And what a mighty anointing the Lord has given Benny Hinn. Miracles and healings galore! Praise God! When the offering was to be taken, the Lord told Benny Hinn to withhold doing so because the Lord wanted to start healing immediately. Benny Hinn said this has never happened to him before in his entire ministry, but he flowed with the Holy Spirit and did not grieve the Holy Spirit. He obeyed the Spirit rather than his own mind. Benny was told to hold up the offering for well over an hour, during which time healings ensued. Praise God!

The anointings of God allow us to do things supernaturally

and to be something we cannot do or be of ourselves as human beings. There are different kinds of anointings, but only one and the same Anointed One, namely, Jesus Christ. In the anointing, God becomes aligned with our human spirits so we in our humanity manifest the deity of God in *action* and in *being*. We distinguish between the *power* and the *presence* of God in us through His anointing. When we *act* by ministering to others, it is God, the Anointed One, who is ministering through us. When we manifest love, joy, peace, patience, etc., within our *being*, it is God, the Anointing One whose presence is being manifested through us. The Holy Spirit is the Spirit of the Son, Jesus, The Anointed One, as Paul describes in Gal. 4:6: ***"Because you are sons, God sent the Spirit of his Son into our hearts, the Spirit who calls out, 'Abba, Father.'"***

We can differentiate between internal and external anointings. The internal anointing is abiding without limit. Jn. 3:34 says, ***"For the one whom God has sent speaks the words of God, for God gives the Spirit without limit."*** Those joined to the Lord become one with His heart and Spirit as it says in 1 Cor. 6:17: ***"But he who unites himself with the Lord is one with him in spirit."*** In 2 Sam. 3:11, we see this abiding anointing both increasing and decreasing respectively in David's and Saul's lives: ***"The war between the house of Saul and the house of David lasted a long time. David grew stronger and stronger, while the house of Saul grew weaker and weaker."*** The external anointing, on the other hand, is a passing, "pouring out" anointing that comes as needed for ministry and then leaves again. Some people describe it as the sensation of oil being poured, a presence of the Lord upon them or a mystical, tingling sensation. 1 Sam. 17:34 tells us David was anointed to kill a bear, a lion and the uncircumcised giant Goliath. David told Saul,

> *Your servant has killed both the lion and the bear; this uncircumcised Philistine will be like one of them, because he has defied the armies of the living God. The LORD who delivered me from the paw of the lion and the paw of the bear will deliver me from the hand of this Philistine.*

Is. 10:27 speaks of this anointing: *"And it shall come to pass in that day, [that] his burden shall be taken away from off thy shoulder, and his yoke from off thy neck, and the yoke shall be destroyed because of the anointing."* [KJV] We can also see different dimensions of the anointing whether it is an individual or a corporate anointing. The individual anointing is described by Paul as *"Christ in you"* in Col. 1:17: *"To whom God would make known what [is] the riches of the glory of this mystery among the Gentiles; which is Christ in you, the hope of glory."* Also, in Rom. 8:10,11:

> *And if Christ [be] in you, the body [is] dead because of sin; but the Spirit [is] life because of righteousness. But if the Spirit of him that raised up Jesus from the dead dwell in you, he that raised up Christ from the dead shall also quicken your mortal bodies by his Spirit that dwelleth in you.*

The corporate anointing is plural; it is meant for the Body of Christ operating as members of one another in a team concept of ministry.

In summary, the internal anointing is a calling on one's life to accomplish the purposes and plans of God, such as the anointing to spoil or the anointing for intercession. The external anointing is the presence of the Holy Spirit that enables one to minister as the Spirit leads.

The anointing has manifested in my life in various ways. On Wednesday, March 25, 1992, at our prayer group, one brother shared a revelation the Lord had given him in Eph. 1:15-23:

> *I pray that . . . you may know . . . his incomparably great power for us who believe. That power . . . which he exerted in Christ when he raised him from the dead and seated him at his right hand in the heavenly realms.*

WE HAVE THAT SAME POWER! THE SAME RESURRECTION POWER THAT RAISED CHRIST FROM THE DEAD! JESUS WANTS ALL OF US TO USE THAT POWER! Eph. 1:23 says, *"God placed all things under his feet and appointed him to be head over everything for the church, which is his body."*

HE HAS GIVEN US THE SAME POWER![276]

> *Then Jesus came to them and said, "All authority in heaven and on earth has been given to me.*

---

[276] Lk. 9:1: When Jesus had called the Twelve together, he gave them power and authority to drive out all demons and to cure diseases, 2 and he sent them out to preach the kingdom of God and to heal the sick.
Lk. 10:19: 9 I have given you authority to trample on snakes and scorpions and to overcome all the power of the enemy; nothing will harm you.

Therefore go and make disciples of all nations, baptizing them in the name of the Father and of the Son and of the Holy Spirit, and teaching them to obey everything I have commanded you. And surely I am with you always, to the very end of the age. [277]

One of my friends, who was to accompany me on the business trip, stopped by in the evening. We went out for supper to make specific plans for the California trip. He felt that Proverbs 16:9 was significant in planning for this trip: *"In his heart a man plans his course, but the Lord determines his steps."* Thank you, Jesus! Praise the Lord!

The following day as a group of us were in prayer, doubts and fear began coming against me while I prayed. So in the name of Jesus and by His authority I took the demons head on and they fled. I received peace, and after we waited upon the Lord for several minutes, He spoke to me: *"When your desires are in perfect harmony with Mine, I will always grant your desires."* Then, as I thought of the California project, the Lord said, *"Go now, for I have commissioned you to do My Work."* One brother gave me Joshua 1:3: *"I will give you every place where you set your foot, as I promised Moses."*

This scripture applied to more than the California project. For the spiritual battle to be fought is a territorial one. We claim and take every territory taken from us or promised to us for God's kingdom. Praise God.

Another brother shared what the Lord impressed upon him

---

[277] Mt. 28:18

from Jer. 9:23: ***"This is what the Lord says: 'Let not the wise man boast of his wisdom or the strong man boast of his strength or the rich man boast of his riches.'"*** Listen to what God says; do not be impressed so much by what men do!

Also, Jer. 7:22-23 says,

For when I brought your forefathers out of Egypt and spoke to them, I did not just give them commands about burnt offerings and sacrifices, but I gave them this command: Obey me, and I will be your God and you will be my people. Walk in all the ways I command you, that it may go well with you.

God is looking for a human vessel that has availability, not ability. Listen to God!

One other brother told me to read 3 John in preparation for the trip. Suddenly, after reading that short book for several days, the following jumped as a rhema[278] word: ***WALK IN THE TRUTH; BE FAITHFUL IN WHAT YOU ARE DOING; FOR THE SAKE OF THE NAME GO OUT.*** The Lord told me, ***"With humble and pure hearts you are to seek the Lord's counsel; honor Him. Keep the boundaries intact by the Lord's protection; claim it for the Lord."***

The following Scripture passages were given to us: ***"In his***

---

[278] A rhema is a word that appears to become enlarged or to jump off the page at a person, coming alive and having a relevant meaning for that person at that time.

heart a man plans his course, but the Lord determines his steps;"[279] *"How much better to get wisdom than gold, to choose understanding rather than silver;"*[280] *"'For I am coming, and I will live among you,' declares the Lord. 'Many nations will be joined with the Lord in that day and will become my people. I will live among you and you will know that the Lord Almighty has sent me to you;'"*[281] *"'Not by might nor by power, but by My Spirit,' says the Lord Almighty;"*[282] and *"Since the Spirit is our life, let us be led by the Spirit."*[283]

If more people understood the purpose of the anointing, more would desire it. We simply cannot do spiritual supernatural works in our own strength. We need the anointing of the Anointed One.

But you have an anointing from the Holy One, and all of you know the truth. . . . As for you, the anointing you received from him remains in you, and you do not need anyone to teach you. But as his anointing teaches you about all things and as that anointing is real, not counterfeit—just as it has taught you, remain in him.[284]

On Friday morning, March 27, 1992, I experienced a powerful anointing. One of the intercessors who was a pastor joined

---

[279] Pr. 16:9
[280] Pr. 16:16
[281] Zech. 2:10,11
[282] Zech 2:6
[283] Gal. 5:25
[284] 1 Jn. 2:20,27

my then Catholic pastor and myself at the *Fanning the Flame Seminar* at Sacred Heart School of Theology. Praise God! The Lord is doing a mighty move of His Spirit in some areas in the Catholic Church. Many priests, seminarians, lay people and pastors of various denominations attended the talk entitled, *Fanning The Flame,* by Fathers George Montague and Killian McDonnell. The Holy Spirit was present and moving, hovering over the meeting. Hallelujah! Thank God!

CHAPTER 17

Seeking Jesus

On Wednesday morning, April 22, 1992, at 10 o'clock, a brother picked me up and we drove to Cedar Rapids, Iowa, for "A Time To Seek God" Spring Leadership Conference, with Francis Frangipane and Reuven Doron as the keynote speakers. On the way there, this brother had me read Proverbs 3 aloud, putting my name in every verse as though the Lord was speaking to me personally. What an awesome experience! Try it, dear reader! In each verse and wherever it says "My son," put your name there instead. He also told me that I was to read 1 Pet. 3:8-4:13 regarding the "good friends" who came to advise me as they advised Job. Praise God!

We arrived in time for the 3:30 P.M. session at River of Life Worship Center. My perceptions, reflections and thoughts of the highlights of these talks and the praise and worship are summarized below. Just let them minister to your spirit as they did to mine.

Francis Frangipane gave the first talk after praise and worship, entitled *Seeking God.* All we need is God. Outside of His fullness, we need nothing more! When we possess Him, Scripture tells us that *"His glory will be seen upon [us]."* [285] A hunger for holiness leads to repentance. The only way to receive the fullness of His glory is through the spirit of repentance, which is the spirit of Elijah. In Mt. 17:11, Jesus said the

---

[285] Is. 60:2

spirit of Elijah **RESTORES** all things; it brings change into the hearts of people. But this change of heart is blocked by a lack of repentance, which hinders God's glory and power. The voice of the Lord must be recognized today as it was 2,000 years ago when John the Baptist said, ***"I am the voice of the one [God] crying in the wilderness."***[286] I pray we discern that voice of God in the wilderness, which is a call to repentance. John the Baptist remained in the desert, yet people from many places sought him out. It is believed he baptized 750,000 to 1,000,000 people who were willing to repent.

Repentance is not saying, "I'm sorry," but saying, "I'm ready!" It's not my way or your way, but Yahweh! Is. 40:3 says, ***"A voice of one calling: Clear the way, the Lord is coming."*** Pride and hurts are obstacles to the glory of the Lord being revealed. Pride is a mountain; hurts can be valleys! "Every mountain made low and every valley lifted up"[287] means all pride is crushed and all hurts are healed!

The 7 P.M. talk by Francis Frangipane was entitled ***Secret Place of the Most High.*** Francis exclaimed, "I'm coming to you, Lord, even if I'm the biggest hypocrite; I'm coming to you just as I am. Only You can change me to be a holy habitation for You! ***"For we are the temple of the living God."***[288] God is within us! In Heb. 9:8 God says, ***"The Holy of Holies"*** is within us (inner tabernacle). The outer court is the vain, ego-centered soul-life, that must be broken, shattered by the Lord upon repentance—a hunger for holiness. We must yield ourselves to the Lord for only He can do the mighty work of holiness in us. Read

---

[286] Jn. 1:23

[287] Is. 40:4

[288] 2 Cor. 6:16

Song of Songs 2:8-9 to grasp the hunger of the Beloved for the Lover:

> *Listen! My lover! Look! Here he comes, leaping across the mountains, bounding over the hills. My lover is like a gazelle or a young stag. Look! There he stands behind our wall, gazing through the windows, peering through the lattice.*

Look what Ps. 24:3-6 says about who can enter into the holy place, the secret place of the Most High God: *"Who may ascend the hill of the Lord? Who may stand [called by the Lord] in His holy place? He who has clean hands and a pure heart, who does not lift up his soul to an idol or swear by what is false."* Whatever sin and imperfections we were able to get away with in the outer court will get us killed and fried in the inner court, the Holy of Holies. We can enter the inner court only with a pure, repentant heart, for there is no sin in the presence of God, who is a *"consuming fire."*[289] We need to turn our obstinate will toward God and exclaim, "Deliver me, O Lord! I yield myself to You. Make me holy even as You are holy!"[290]

The purpose of the Holy Spirit is to lead us to Jesus, who brings us to the secret place, where signs and wonders will follow. The signs and wonders of the early church were recorded in *The Book of Acts*. If we recorded today's church activities, we would have to call it *The Book of Tries* (instead of Acts). Where are the signs and wonders following the disciples of Jesus today?

---

[289] Heb. 12:29: For our God [is] a consuming fire.
[290] Rev. 4:8: "Holy, holy, holy is the Lord God Almighty, who was, and is, and is to come."

Whatever obstacles are hindering God from moving through us must be identified and removed. One major obstacle to getting into His presence is when we say, "God, why don't you use me?" That spirit of rejection and self-pity has to come out of its hiding place with its hands up and surrender! Once we get rid of all obstacles, we can enter into His presence. We must listen to God and have him tell us what we need to do in order to enter into His Presence! Everyone who seeks, finds![291] When we seek Him, He will not deny us.

On Thursday, April 23, 1992, Reuven Doron gave a talk entitled *Touch the Lord, and Produce Fruit.* His message focused on the iniquity within that must be identified and removed. Clean out the old leaven or it will permeate the whole loaf. In Jn. 20:17 Jesus said, ***"Stop clinging to me, for I have not ascended to my Father."*** But as soon as He sat at the right hand of the Father, He said, ***"Come, touch Me!"*** Jesus wants us to draw near to Him; He is our intercessor before the Throne of grace. Jesus is calling us into a deep relationship with the Father as in Ps. 42:7: ***"Deep calls to deep in the roar of your waterfalls."*** Gen. 7:11 says the windows of heaven are opened and the fountains below spring up! God waters us with His grace from every direction when we draw near to Him. When God moves, He moves mightily! He floods us with blessings from above and below. Ps. 133 tells us God desires unity with us; He wants harmony with us. Touch Him! The Lord is not too lofty that He cannot be touched by a humble heart. Ps. 100:4 encourages us to ***"enter His gates with thanksgiving."*** Is. 57:15 says of the Lord, ***"I live in a high and holy place, but also with him who is contrite and lowly in spirit."***

---

[291] Lk. 11:10; Mt 7:8: 8 For everyone who asks receives; he who seeks finds; and to him who knocks, the door will be opened.

There are different ways of touching the Lord. We see this in the faith of Peter, the love of John, the touch of the woman with the issue of blood. *"Come to Me for I am meek and humble of heart."* [292] Jn. 3:18-21 assures us that we have access to Him *"if our hearts do not condemn us."* [293] Touch the Lord and and you will produce fruit.

At 1 P.M. on April 23rd, Francis Frangipane entitled his talk *Seeking Jesus is to be a Normal Experience.* For every Christian, seeking Jesus is to be a normal experience in every situation and opportunity presented to us. We need to say, "I'm looking for the Lord! Anything else is poverty! I'm reaching, standing on my tip-toes, reaching for Him. Make me your complete servant." James 4:5 says the Spirit He has caused to live in us envies intensely. God wants our attention and affection! Then, He will do mighty things through us. Jesus only did what He saw the Father doing, therefore, everything Jesus commanded, happened. We are not to strive to believe more, but to see more clearly in order to operate as Jesus did. Purity of heart is a closeness to Jesus that will give us clearer vision to see the Father.

The human spirit is a complex one to understand. If we have given God our human spirit, He has all of us: our soul, our body and our spirit. If God controls our spirit, we are great in His sight! Pr. 16:32 says, *"Greater is he who controls his spirit than one who takes (conquers) a city."* Also, Pr. 25:28 says, *"Like a city whose walls are broken into (down) is a man who has no control over his spirit."* Discipline over our soul, body and spirit will lead to victory; lack of discipline

---

[292] Mt. 11:29
[293] 2 Cor. 6:11; Pr. 17:3; Phil. 1:29

will lead to destruction. The enemy comes in masquerading as your thoughts. We can reject the enemy's attacks by taking every thought captive unto Jesus Christ.[294] Then Pr. 20:27 will become reality in us: *"The lamp of the Lord searches the spirit of a man."* Is. 57:15 confirms the conditions for having the presence of the God of light. The *"contrite"* of heart are *"revived,"* having the presence of God. Before going to sleep at night, position your spirit in the presence of Jesus. 1 Cor. 2:10 assures us *"the Spirit searches all things, even the depths of God."* One response to God's presence to us is our powerful worship of Him. The Lord is saying, "The contrite of spirit are the ones I esteem."[295]

Ambition, distractions, anxiety preclude finding Jesus. We all want to be successful. Success is striving to remain little (not looking for pre-eminence). Success is being united to God and striving to see Him. Mt. 18:3 says, *"Whosoever humbles himself like this child is the greatest in the kingdom of heaven."* [KJV] That's success! Reverse your trend of thought. The world has nothing to offer in comparison. Surrender to the Lord: "Lord, I'm your servant. *'So you also, when you have done everything you were told to do, should say, "We are unworthy servants; we have only done our duty."'*[296] I am pleasing to you, Lord. I don't dare compare myself with anyone else. Shape me, Lord, for your dwelling place. I'm being

---

[294] 2 Cor. 10:5,6: We demolish arguments and every pretension that sets itself up against the knowledge of God, and we take captive every thought to make it obedient to Christ. 6 And we will be ready to punish every act of disobedience, once your obedience is complete.

[295] Ps. 51:17: The sacrifices of God are a broken spirit; a broken and contrite heart, O God, you will not despise.

[296] Lk. 17:5-10

prepared to see my Jesus! Direct me to You! Put a new song in my heart! Come and consume me, that You may be seen in me by others."[297]

Following his talk, the words of one of the songs we sung touched me deeply: "Give us rivers in the desert, let them over-flow. Send your rain (a Biblical word for abundant blessings), send your rain! Pour out your Spirit! Water all the earth. Fill us with Your power. Flood us with Your light. Soften with Your showers 'till our hearts are owned by You. The outpouring of Your Spirit, for Your streams are full of power. Send your rain!" This is the abundant grace offered to us as we seek Him.

At 7 P.M. Reuven Doron spoke on *The Presence of the Lord.* Ps.76:1-3 declares, *"God is known in Judah; His name is great in Israel. His tent is in Salem, His dwelling place in Zion."* Ex. 33:13 says, *"My Presence will go with you, and I will give you rest."* Mt. 7:7 says, *"Ask and it will be given to you; seek and you will find; knock and it will be opened to you."* There are degrees of seeking (finding) the Lord, degrees of entry into God: Ask, seek and knock. These are degrees of God's Presence! They are deter-mined by our level of persistence when pressing into His pres-ence. In Ex. 24:9-18, Moses went up and saw the God of Israel. He left everything behind! In Ex. 20, the people trembled at God and feared Him. They feared the manifestation of His holy Presence. Contrary to Moses, a seeker of God, the people were afraid of Him because they did not know Him. They saw Him as dangerous and stayed away, asking Moses to speak to God on

---

[297] Is. 66:2: The nations will see your righteousness, and all kings your glory; you will be called by a new name that the mouth of the LORD will bestow.

their behalf.[298]   Religion was born, putting distance between the Israelites and God! But in Ex. 32, the people went insane without being in the Presence of God! They made an idol and worshipped what they did not fear. We must worship God or we will go insane with our idols and remain in deception.[299]

These are our options: His Presence or our insanity! So be encouraged to Ask, Seek, and Knock! Jesus is immediate! Today! Now! If we don't have the Presence of God today, we have nothing! In Is. 36:1-38, King Hezekiah entered the temple of the Lord and knocked and the Lord delivered him and his nation. He was desperate to have God!

Then, Reuven told the story of his involvement in the Battle of the Golan Heights in 1976 when he, as an Israeli officer, led 60 men into an ambush! But, oh, how the Lord used that incident in his life! Reuven knew he had divine protection from the enemy's bullets and, though he did not personally know the Lord at that time, Reuven knew God had plans for him in the future, reflective of Jer. 29:11-13: *"I know the plans I have for you."* Lord, help us all find You and the destiny You have for each of us!

When we dive deeply into God, we remove the defenses

---

[298] Ex. 20:18-21: When the people saw the thunder and lightning and heard the trumpet and saw the mountain in smoke, they trembled with fear. They stayed at a distance 19 and said to Moses, "Speak to us yourself and we will listen. But do not have God speak to us or we will die." 20 Moses said to the people, "Do not be afraid. God has come to test you, so that the fear of God will be with you to keep you from sinning." 21 The people remained at a distance, while Moses approached the thick darkness where God was. 22 Then the LORD said to Moses, "Tell the Israelites this: 'You have seen for yourselves that I have spoken to you from heaven: 23 Do not make any gods to be alongside me; do not make for yourselves gods of silver or gods of gold.'"

[299] Ex. 32:1-4

protecting us from the dangerous, unpredictable God! God is dangerous and unpredictable to our comfortable lives when we yield everything to Him. We step out of our comfort zones and trust the Lord, who is faithful to His word and receives our total commitment. Take me into the Holy of Holies; take me in by the blood of the Lamb![300]

A song that followed again moved my soul: "More love, more power, more of You in my life! In the presence of Your glory, As I cry: 'Holy, Holy, Holy God.' How awesome is Your name, Holy, Holy, Holy God; How majestic is Your name. I am changed in the Presence of a holy God."

Francis Frangipane then had a prophecy: **You are my holy ground and I shall rain upon you.** Praise God! I received this word for myself! This confirmed the shower of grace that the Lord was pouring out upon His people.

On Friday, April 24th, 1992, at 9 A.M. Francis Frangipane spoke on *Becoming Desperate in Passionately Seeking Jesus.* The feminine side of Christ (such as the gifts of helps ministry, compassion, counsel, etc.) has been dominant in the Church. The masculine side of Christ (warrior, intercessor, king, etc.) is growing in the Church today. The spiritual authority of doing warfare should not replace the intimate relationship with Christ. There has to be a balance. We need an ever increasing presence of God in our life. Our programs cannot do what only God can do. Ps. 53:2 reminds us that **"God looks down from heaven . . . to see if there are . . . any who seek God."** Jesus drew His strength from God every day. He had a relentless hunger to seek God! Song of Songs 3:1 is a story of the spiritual reality of the

---

[300] Rev. 12:11

bride seeking the love of the bridegroom.

We can either pass through the invisible barrier, the narrow path eliminating the distance between God and man (presence of God) and seek Him until we break through, or we can adjust our doctrine to a comfortable stage where God is in His heaven and we stay comfortable here on earth. But then we never really know Him. The reality of His Presence must be as visible and real as the world was before we knew Him.

In Song of Songs 3:2, the bride puts away her fears and becomes vulnerable in seeking the bridegroom. When your love of God overcomes your fear of the enemy, you can do spiritual warfare. The command is: Come to me all you who are burdened![301] We can come boldly into His throne of grace.[302] But only the pure of heart can see God.[303]

This search for God is a pilgrimage. Repentance for areas holding us back is necessary. This is not a matter of discipline, but of desire. Song of Songs 3:3 asks us if we have seen Jesus. The watchmen are like the prophetic ministry; they give us signposts to Jesus. Song of Songs 3:4 says, ***"Scarcely had I passed them when I found the one my heart loves. I held him and would not let him go."*** Now is the time when we are able to find Him if we truly seek Him.

---

[301] Mt. 11:28: "Come to me, all you who are weary and burdened, and I will give you rest. 29 Take my yoke upon you and learn from me, for I am gentle and humble in heart, and you will find rest for your souls. 30 For my yoke is easy and my burden is light."

[302] Heb. 4: 16: Let us then approach the throne of grace with confidence, so that we may receive mercy and find grace to help us in our time of need.

[303] Mt. 5:8: Blessed are the pure in heart, for they will see God.

A spirit-filled Christian is likened to a power plant, not a dust-filled museum. When we want God the same way our lungs want air, we will find Him. Jn. 20:1-18 shows us Mary seeking Jesus at the empty tomb. We must maintain our focus on Jesus. The charismatic Church is impressed with angels; the Bride Church is only impressed with Jesus. "Woman, whom are you seeking?"[304] Song of Songs 4:9 admits, *"You have stolen my heart with one glance of your eyes."* Jesus is coming back, not so much to judge, but to receive His Bride who passionately seeks Him.

In the afternoon, after praise and worship, there was a short prophecy by Francis Frangipane:

You are not alone today, yesterday or tomorrow. Even as I have brought you this far, I will bring you to Me. Your desire for Me is only a faint echo of My desire for you. I have brought you here to plant you, water you and weed you. And I am sending you back with the tools! And my arm is not short!

Hallelujah! Lord, I seek your face, not your hands!

The Friday afternoon session was a series of diverse questions that were answered by Francis Frangipane, Reuven Doron and Marvin Eales.[305] The reader may find this session very helpful as a prototype of a truly spiritual church. See **Appendix D**.

---

[304] Jn. 20:15: "Woman," he said, "why are you crying? Who is it you are looking for?"

[305] All were pastors at River of Life Church in Cedar Rapids, IA.

On Friday evening, Francis Frangipane gave a teaching entitled ***Desire Fulfilled.*** We have an unconscious quest for fulfillment. Prov. 13:12 says, ***"Hope deferred makes the heart sick, but a longing [a desire] fulfilled is a tree of life."*** We want to be drawn to the place where hope is fulfilled—in Jesus Christ.

In Gen. 29:16, the story of Leah and Rachael shows Jacob loved Rachael and Leah was hated. The Lord saw that Leah was unloved and He gave her Reuben: ***"Surely my husband will love me now."*** But she was unfulfilled. After giving birth to Simeon and Levi, she still was not loved and fulfilled. In verse 35, Leah was changed inside; she thought, "Even if my husband doesn't love me, ***'this time I will praise the Lord'*** with Judah." Leah started looking in the right place for fulfillment, which was the Lord. In Gen. 48:29, it tells us God continued to do a work in her life. In her old age, she found fulfillment in her husband, for Jacob on his deathbed said that along with his ancestors, Abraham and Sarah, Isaac and Rebekah, ***"there I buried Leah"*** (not Rachael).

It is you, Lord, we are sincerely seeking for true fulfillment. In this life I will praise the Lord—the reason for my existence. This day I will praise the Lord; I will commit my life to God today; I purpose my life to give praise to God! And you, Lord, be my fulfillment and my tree of life.

CHAPTER 18

Love Covers All—Victory!

There was a season when I experienced the accuser of the brethren spreading strong calumny and detraction against me. The Lord was allowing me to deal with this to build me up to have the mind and heart of Christ toward my enemies. *"But I tell you who hear me: Love your enemies, do good to those who hate you, bless those who curse you, pray for those who mistreat you."* [306] This is not easy, but it certainly kills the flesh and brings it into submission if we do not yield to the temptation to lash back.

On Tuesday morning, June 2, 1992 as I read Scripture in a restaurant, Hosea 12:6 was given to me: *"But you must return to your God; maintain love and justice; and wait for your God always."* I sensed that the Lord was asking me and all others to constantly repent, to have a change of mind so powerful it changes the course of action. I made an act of faith! And though I was to wait for the Lord's movement, I sensed strongly that the Lord is now moving! I await the Lord's move!

At the office I spoke to an intercessor and proclaimed Is. 60 with her via phone. We again talked about the word she had received regarding me a year ago, and I am awed at the depth of the concepts: *You are a member of my royal priesthood in the order of Melchizedek, a chosen man, chosen like none other.*

Another intercessor phoned and had a word for the day:

[306]   Lk. 6:27,28

"Faith works by patience." [307] The Lord was building up my faith so I can stand strong before the enemy. *"My righteous one will live by faith."* [308] *"His faithfulness will be your shield and rampart."* [309]

At our prayer meeting, after proclaiming Is. 60 aloud, four of us anointed with oil and prayed over one brother for the Lord's clear direction in his life and ministry, and full use of his gifts for the Lord's kingdom. Another intercessor phoned to give me a rhema that jumped out at her as she was praying for me and the Company; the Scripture passage was in Job 8:7: *"Your beginnings will seem humble, so prosperous will your future be."* Praise the Lord!

I was just practicing perfect patience, waiting upon the Lord for His movement, and attempting to put myself into His perfect will! Another brother phoned and asked that I read Job for encouragement regarding what I was going through. Praise God!

On Thursday morning, June 4, 1992, I was reading *Deep Calleth Deep* by Richard Gazowsky in Chapter VII, The Art of War, where he says that we are to take the time to make past mistakes right; bind up all hurts we may have left behind and heal those relationships lest we make ourselves vulnerable to an attack by satan in the future. Praise God! I immediately thought of writing to Bishop Cletus O'Donnell, my former bishop in the Diocese of Madison, and making certain that all hurts between us are healed. Praise God!

---

[307] Gal. 5:5

[308] Heb. 12:38

[309] Ps. 91:4

I went to the office and wrote and sent the following letter to Bishop O'Donnell:

Laverne C. Ihm
2627 N. 114th Street
Wauwatosa, WI 53226
June 4, 1992

Reverend Cletus F. O'Donnell
Bishop of the Diocese of Madison
15 E. Wilson Street
Madison, WI 53702

Dear Bishop O'Donnell:

I pray this letter will find you in improving health. I have heard that you have had some serious health problems and I pray the Lord is giving you the strength you need to withstand these trying circumstances, knowing full well that reality is not what circumstances may appear to be, but reality is what God is doing in our lives!

Our faith, the eyesight of our spirit, tells us that the glory of the Lord will come forth through us (Isaiah 60), and the things of this earth, including all powers and riches of this earth, shall be destroyed. Praise God!

Bishop, I am writing to you today, not only to encourage you, but also to make certain that there exists between us no unforgiveness of the past, no bitterness and no hurts unhealed. I ask your forgiveness for anything I have done against you or Madison Diocese in leaving the active ministry, and I hold no bitterness, hurts or unforgiveness against you or anyone in the Diocese of Madison. I forgive all in the name of Jesus and ask the same forgiveness by all.

Today I was reading a book by Richard Gazowsky, **Deep Calleth Deep**; he counsels all of us to take the time to make past mistakes or hurts right; to bind up all hurts we may have left behind and heal those relationships, lest we make ourselves very vulnerable to an attack by satan in the future.

I have been called to a ministry of intercessory prayer, Bishop, and as the Lord Jesus passionately draws me closer and closer to His heart, seeking Him and Him alone, the Lord has revealed areas in my life from which I need deliverance and healing, so He can enter in fully. I thank the Lord for His mercy and kindness.

Twice every week on Wednesday and Friday noon until 1 P.M. many of us businessmen and women get together in my office to pray and praise the Lord. The Lord has blessed these prayer group members with His blessings of love, joy, peace, patience, kindness, gentleness, faithfulness, goodness and fear of the Lord.

The Spirit of the Lord has used this small group by calling it to do His work of preaching good news to the poor, binding up the brokenhearted, proclaiming freedom for the captives, releasing from darkness the prisoners, proclaiming the year of the Lord's favor and the day of vengeance of our God, comforting all who mourn, and providing for those who grieve in Zion, because the Spirit of the Sovereign Lord is upon us (Is. 61:1-3).

I thank the Lord for what He is doing in our lives! What a mighty God we serve! Praise Him!

May Jesus' love be powerful in your life!

Sincerely,

Laverne C. Ihm

When I got back from Kentucky on June 19th, I read the letter from Bishop O'Donnell, written painstakingly with his left hand since his right hand was paralyzed by a stroke.

Office of the Bishop
Diocese of Madison
P. O. Box 111
15 East Wilson Street
Madison, Wisconsin 53701
June 12, 1992

Dear Laverne,

It was good to hear from you after these many years. I suffered a severe stroke last October. I appreciate your words of encouragement and I am grateful to you. I have nothing against you. You seem to have it all together. In the past years I have prayed for you and will continue to do so.

Peace,

Bishop O'Donnell
P.S.: Hope you can read this.

God not only wants us to deal with current enemies, but He wants us to rectify all past separations and divisions.

If I offend you today, you say I need to repent and apologize. If ten years pass by, would you say that time has done away with the need to repent and apologize? No. What about 20 years? No. Time does not do away with the need to repent for sin and the need to be reconciled. Forgotten sins that have not been repented for do not go away with the passage of time. This is true for individual sin as well as national and generational sins of the past. Reconciliation is love restored which covers a multitude of sins! When I, along with three other brothers, visited a brother in Pagosa Springs, Colorado, on April 2, 1992, I was delivered of the generational curse of anger.

The Lord had previously told me we would bless and be blessed with an infilling of His Presence and anointing while in Pagosa Springs with Peter and Rebekah Laue. We arrived at their home, The Hiding Place, and were taken to the Upper Room immediately. Peter greeted and hugged each of us! He started talking and walking back and forth, saying, "God is giving us more keys! He is giving us more keys! To set the captives free! Mercy is God's dominant nature!"

Then Peter told us about how he fought the spirit of anger and all of its many manifestations, sarcasm, innuendoes, negative insinuations, unkind compliments, etc.[310] I spoke up and confessed that I, too, wanted to rid myself of this same spirit of anger and its manifestations. One brother told me the Lord revealed to him *that this was an ancestral sin, passed down for generations! My father had it, my grandfather had it, but it will not be passed to my descendants.*[311] Praise the Lord!

---

[310] This confession later appeared in his public ministry newsletter.

[311] We were dealing with iniquity of sin here, the residue of the devil that remains in the soulish realm after the spirit has been cleansed from sin through repentance. It is this iniquity that must be purged so the devil has no hold on us! Much of this iniquity is generational, handed down from one generation to another. But the anointing can break the yoke over us and our posterity. We can break the cycle of passing on generational sin and curses now! Since that day I have not struggled with anger or losing my temper. I am free! I am delivered! Hallelujah!

Peter said that the only way of delivering myself of this spirit of anger was to profess with my tongue that I am determined to crush and repudiate the spirit of anger and any of its manifestations in Jesus' Name. I gladly professed, "I am determined in Jesus' Name to repudiate and deliver myself from the spirit of anger and any of its manifestations." Peter asked that I share with my wife and daughter this profession of determination when I returned home. Praise the Lord!

One of the men had a vision of **the Lord holding the spirit of anger in the palm of His Hand and with His Thumb the Lord crushed the devil and destroyed his power as I professed those words with my tongue.** Praise God! Since that time I have not had the struggle of trying to control my temper. That iniquity was removed! Praise the Lord!

CHAPTER 19

The Divine Umbilical Cord

On the evening of September 22, 1992, I went to a Pipeline to Jesus prayer meeting. Jim Partington was preaching and ministering. After praise and worship there were two words spoken.

The first was a tongue message through a lady, which was interpreted by Ron Gartner, a missionary who had just arrived back from the Philippines:

Do you not know I am in your midst? I am among you, within you! Seek Me! Do you not know Something Greater than material things is among you? Do you not know that Something Greater than entertainment is among you? Seek Me and all your needs will be met. For I am God Almighty!

Then, immediately following, another word was spoken by another person: *"Be strong in the time of trial now necessary to deliver the land. I ask you to remember to pray for the leaders I have chosen over your country. The land I have given you is holy land. And remember I love you!"*

Annette Damico, the leader of the meeting, quoted Eph. 1:16-18: *"Cease not to give thanks,"* and prayed for several people, mentioning that we should especially remember our families as in Is. 42:26: *"Put the Lord in remembrance."*

Then Jim Partington talked on *The Return of Christ: HE*

IS COMING BACK! Though the Holy Spirit works through willing vessels, spiritual gifts are not in themselves a mark of maturity! Spiritual gifts are given for ministry to others, not as a sign of one's holiness! He read Rev. 2:2-3:

> *I know your deeds, your hard work and your perseverance. I know that you cannot tolerate wicked men, that you have tested those who claim to be apostles but are not, and have found them false. You have persevered and have endured hardships for my name, and have not grown weary.*

Then he commented, "The Holy Spirit works through you; He lives in you. The hardest thing to do is nothing! It is more important to be than to do! Let the Holy Spirit do His work in you. God is moving. You won't miss God if you are available."

Jim gave an allegory of a violin player who was not very good with the violin, but when a professional asked if he could place himself inside the amateur, though it looked like the amateur was playing, the music was sweet and awesome. "Let the Holy Spirit take you over and place Himself inside you to play the violin!"

He gave us a series of Scriptures regarding the Second Coming of Christ: 2 Pet. 1:3; Acts 1:11; I Cor. 1:7; Phil. 3:20; Ti. 2:13; 1 Thess. 5:6-8; 1 Jn. 3:3; Ps. 45; Ps. 60; 1 Thess. 9:10; Rev. 3:10 and Heb. 9:28. The *"first love"*[312] forsaken by the Church of Ephesus, which Jesus held against them, was forsaking *"the*

---

[312] Rev. 2:4

living hope of the return of Jesus."[313] The Ephesian Church forsook their first love. But Jesus is coming back! The Holy Spirit is alive! He is working in us now!

Then Jim told a story about the concern and interest of the Holy Spirit in little matters as well as big things in our lives! *"Seek first the kingdom of God and all these things will be added to you."*[314]

We have not been called to religion, but to spirituality. There is a big difference between the two. God is interested in a intimate relationship with us, not in us keeping a bunch of rules. *"Religion that God our Father accepts as pure and faultless is this: to look after orphans and widows in their distress and to keep oneself from being polluted by the world."*[315] In Jn. 15:15-17 Jesus said,

> *I no longer call you servants, because a servant does not know his master's business. Instead, I have called you friends, for everything that I learned from my Father I have made known to you. You did not choose me, but I chose you and appointed you to go and bear fruit—fruit that will last. Then the Father will give you whatever you ask in my name. This is my command: Love each other.*

Notice Jesus said, *"I have called you."* God is alive and is involved with you! It isn't that I do nothing; it is that I sit back

---

[313] 1 Pet. 1:3
[314] Mt. 6:33
[315] Jas. 1:27

and watch Him do everything!

Jim had a prophetic word over me from the Lord:

Hallelujiah! Hallelujiah! For the Lord thy God shall straighten out all that is crooked, all that is twisted, all that is tangled, all intrigue, and there shall be a straight and untrammeled [316] wire that shall communicate to thee; there shall be a divine umbilical cord that shall link thy God to thyself, and there shall be a flow of power into thy life. It shall not be manipulated by thee; it shall not be ordained by thee; it shall be ordained by thy God, and thou shall rejoice in all that thy God doeth. Thou shall be a word that is a completion; there is a fulfillment of the purposes of the Lord thy God in thy life. [317]

He paused, and then prayed:

Hallelujah! Hallelujah! Amen. Lord, I pray that

---

[316] An untrammeled wire means an unimpeded or not intercepted communication wire like a direct clear telephone line.

[317] I later thought Jesus' words in Jn. 15:5-11 applied: "I am the vine; you are the branches. If a man remains in me and I in him, he will bear much fruit; apart from me you can do nothing. 6 If anyone does not remain in me, he is like a branch that is thrown away and withers; such branches are picked up, thrown into the fire and burned. 7 If you remain in me and my words remain in you, ask whatever you wish, and it will be given you. 8 This is to my Father's glory, that you bear much fruit, showing yourselves to be my disciples. 9 "As the Father has loved me, so have I loved you. Now remain in my love. 10 If you obey my commands, you will remain in my love, just as I have obeyed my Father's commands and remain in his love. 11 I have told you this so that my joy may be in you and that your joy may be complete.

You be very close to my brother this night. May he realize, Lord, that he has received a touch from the Living God. Lord, may he realize that he has heard Your Voice speaking above the noise that has so occupied him during the day. Lord, Your still small Voice is still speaking.[318] *We thank You, Lord, that it accomplishes Thy Word whereto You send it; it does not return unto You void.*[319] *Amen! Hallelujah! Amen! Bless You! Bless You, brother! Thank you, Lord!*

Indeed, prophecy is given for comfort, edification and exhortation! I received all three that night plus encouragement and joy! Praise the Lord! He is so good! I had such a spirit of joy!

On Wednesday, September 23, 1992, I was impressed by Is. 8:17: *"I will wait for the Lord . . . I will put my trust in him,"* Is. 9:3: *"You have enlarged the nation and increased their joy; they rejoice before you as people rejoice at the harvest, as men rejoice when dividing the plunder,"* and Rev. 19:7: *"Let us rejoice and be glad and give him glory!"*

I received a phone call in the morning from one of the officers of our company telling me that our note for the Company with the bank, which declared bankruptcy earlier, was sold by the Federal Reserve System on auction to a gentleman from Dallas for pennies on a dollar. He further told me that when that man

---

318 1 Kgs. 19:12: After the earthquake came a fire, but the LORD was not in the fire. And after the fire came a gentle whisper [a still small voice in KJV].

319 Is. 55:11: So shall my word be that goeth forth out of my mouth: it shall not return unto me void, but it shall accomplish that which I please, and it shall prosper [in the thing] whereto I sent it. [KJV]

contacts me, we might be able to settle for little or nothing. We might be able to satisfy the entire obligation for as little as $2,000 or less. Praise God!

And that is exactly what happened later. We were forgiven the total obligation! Hallelujah! The Lord was working quickly in response to His word:

> *For the Lord thy God shall straighten out all that is crooked, all that is twisted, all that is tangled, all intrigue, and there shall be a straight and untrammeled wire that shall communicate to thee; there shall be a divine umbilical cord that shall link thy God to thyself, and there shall be a flow of power into thy life.*

One brother shared that as he awoke, the Lord gave him revelation knowledge about Is. 60.[320] Proclaiming it aloud daily over the properties of the Company will not cause or bring about the Force Majeure. To see the daily reciting of Is. 60 as a causative factor in bringing about the Force Majeure or the capitalization of the Company is a ploy or distraction of the enemy. It was as though the Lord was saying: But I gave you the word (regarding Is. 60) so My people will meditate on it and spiritually arise from their bondage! Then all the things in Is. 60 can happen! The Spirit of the Lord rests upon you!

I told the group that the Lord is telling me to obey and trust Him! In His time He will move and get all the credit! Praise God! He wants me to pray, stay in the Word and wait for His

---

[320] We had been proclaiming this Scripture aloud on a regular basis, getting them deep within our spirit.

Mighty Move! Other than that, I cannot figure out where the Holy Spirit wants me to go next, or where He is going to take the Company next! I humbly awaited His orders in submission to His Will!

All this in spite of what some "so-called Christians" say, "Why don't you get a real job so you can pay your bills?" He moved me out of the office and into my home so He could have all my attention, provide for my needs miraculously, and teach me to trust in Him with all my heart and abhor the presumption that the Holy Spirit would automatically bless my plans for the Company!

For I know I must follow the Holy Spirit when He moves, for He does not follow me: *"The wind blows where it wishes and you hear the sound of it, but do not know where it is going; so is everyone who is born of the Spirit."*[321]

Lord, give me the humility and wisdom to know how to follow Your Spirit when He moves. Lord, through that divine umbilical cord You have given me, feed me from the well of living water flowing from the throne room of God.

On Thursday morning, September 24, 1992, I spent time meditating on Is. 60 and related passages, such as Acts 26:17b-18: *"I am sending you to them to open their eyes and turn them from darkness to light, and from the power of Satan to God, so that they may receive forgiveness of sins and a place among those who are sanctified by faith in me,"* and Rev. 21;23-27:

The city does not need the sun or moon to shine on it, for the glory of God gives it light, and the

---

[321] Jn. 3:8

Lamb is its light. The nations will walk by its light, and the kings of the earth will bring their splendor into it. On no day will its gates be shut, for there will be no night there. The glory and honor of the nations will be brought into it. Nothing impure will ever enter it, nor will anyone who does what is shameful or deceitful, but only those whose names are written in the Lamb's book of life."

On Friday, September 25, 1992, at noon I went to our prayer meeting, and was touched by the words of the song: I've got joy like a fountain, I've got love like an ocean, I've got peace like a river in my heart.

The Lord's word prophetically spoken over me about straightening out the crooked applies to more than my situation. The Lord is interested in our entire country and the calling He has given to Americans for the Great Harvest to come. *For the Lord thy God shall straighten out all that is crooked!* So I felt compelled to pray for our country, our land that the Lord says is holy land, and for the leaders, especially the President of the United States that he would be able to speak out with Christian values like those of our founding fathers of this country, and that the Lord could reign in this land! Prayers for repentance, revival and manifestation of His glory were prayed, asking for deliverance from the principalities and powers over our country and city!

One brother had a prophetic word:

I have heard the cry of my people! But that which is of the flesh is flesh, and that which is of the spirit is spirit. I have asked you to crucify the

THE TESTIMONY OF JESUS

flesh. Do not ask Me to change your heart until you are ready to crucify the flesh. Allow the new man to rise up! Let the old man die, and let the new man rise up! [322]

A minister present said the Lord impressed upon him that all the kingdoms rising up against God is but vanity, and they shall fall like pawns when God speaks: "Enough!" When He speaks a judgment on a country it will be done, and when He speaks a blessing on a country, it will be done, for *"The Lord Reigns!"* [323]

Someone passed out a handout with a quote from Rick Joyner's new book: *The Journey Begins*: "Between the place where we receive the promise of God and the Promised Land (the fulfillment of the promise) there is usually going to be a wilderness which is the exact opposite of what we have been promised." How true of every vision the Lord gives us.

---

[322] Rom. 12:2
[323] Ps. 93

CHAPTER 20

I'll Remember the Covenant I Made with You

On Friday, November 6, 1992, the Lord had me read Is. 60:20 and related passages regarding the pillar of cloud and fire. At noon I met with several prayer warriors.

A brother had a prophetic word:

Indeed, I do reign! Trust Me in My word, and abide in My word! To abide means to remain, to live within, to be faithful unto the end, for I want you to reign with Me! And you shall reign if you remain in My word. Abide in Me, and speak forth My word. Let others know the Lord reigns in you. Trust Me.

Then someone present had a word from the Lord:

I will speak to you today. I have not only brought you to a physical place today, but to a spiritual place for My purpose. I call you to not only speak a testimony, but to be a testimony. I call you to walk in the footsteps of righteousness. I am your Lord, and I will not forsake you! I send not just anyone to prison, to the fiery furnace, but only those I can trust. I have called you and ordained you for the fiery furnace not because of what you did wrongly, but for what you did rightfully. My anointing is on you! I am more than your Jehovah Jirah, your Provider, but I am your God! But look to Me not only as your God, but as your Friend, who will not forsake you! You will come out of the furnace of affliction without the smell of smoke on you. I have called you to be the word that will not fail.

In the evening, Jean and I went to Believers' Fellowship Church near Pewaukee to hear Chuck Clayton from Liberty, Indiana, which is on the border of Ohio, 12 miles south of I-70. He is the author of *Accountable Men* and *Faith and the Prophetic*.

His topic was: *I Want To Make a Difference*, and his Scripture was from Rev. 1:13: *"Blessed is he who reads the words of this prophecy, and blessed are those who hear it and take to heart what is written in it, because the time is near."* The Lord doesn't speak to your present, but to your potential, your future. For in Jer. 29:11 the Lord has a plan for us. Jesus said He would reveal His plan to us by His Holy Spirit and today He did by the prophetic message.

Without a vision, My people perish.[324] In Eph. 1:4, God had His plan from the beginning and forever. We must learn to crucify the flesh so we can walk in the Spirit. Tribulations are just for a season.

Lord, show me how to release (my faith in) the fruit of the Spirit. *"I can do all things in him who strengthens me."*[325]

If we receive the word of God for information instead of as

---

[324] Hos. 4:6
[325] Phil. 4:13

a way of life, the devil has just stolen it from our heart. But the devil can't steal the word of God if we put it in our heart instead of our head. We have more faith in Excedrin when we get a headache than we do in His word, but the truth of the word will make you free.[326]

Jesus said the Holy Spirit will **"bring everything to mind that I have told you."** The Holy Spirit is a cheerleader, always encouraging us to remember the Lord's words. Jesus said: Search the Scriptures. God never does anything without His plan. We often try to escape instead of overcome our trials. God says, "I will write my word on your mind and on your heart." If you have a weakness, the Lord will give you trials until you overcome.

Do something about your prophecies; don't just receive them and put them on a shelf. We need to war over them in prayer. Remember how Paul urged Timothy to war over those prophetic words spoken over his life?

Timothy, my son, I give you this instruction in keeping with the prophecies once made about you, so that by following them you may fight the good fight, holding on to faith and a good conscience. Some have rejected these and so have shipwrecked their faith.[327]

---

[326] Jn. 8:31,32: To the Jews who had believed him, Jesus said, "If you hold to my teaching, you are really my disciples. 32 Then you will know the truth, and the truth will set you free."

[327] 1 Tim. 1:10: Timothy, my son, I give you this instruction in keeping with the prophecies once made about you, so that by following them you may fight the good fight, 19 holding on to faith and a good conscience. Some have rejected these and so have shipwrecked their faith.

Sow and you will reap.[328] Sow so much that you can't possibly reap all God has for you in your lifetime, but your children will receive the rest.[329]

Pr. 4:20-22 and Ps. 119:18 urge us to **"know the secret things."** Rev. 2:22 encourages **"renewing our minds."** Revelation is nothing more than a transfer of truth from the word of God to the mind. We must act upon the revelation we receive even as David heeded the word of the prophet and acted upon it in 1 Sam 22:1-5:

David left Gath and escaped to the cave of Adullam. When his brothers and his father's household heard about it, they went down to him there. All those who were in distress or in debt or discontented gathered around him, and he became their leader. About four hundred men were with him. From there David went to Mizpah in Moab and said to the king of Moab, 'Would you let my father and mother come and stay with you until I learn what God will do for me?' So he left them with the king of Moab, and they stayed with him as long as David was in the stronghold. But the prophet Gad said to David, 'Do not stay in the stronghold. Go into the land of Judah.' So David left and went to the forest of Hereth.

---

[328] Gal. 6:7-9: Do not be deceived: God cannot be mocked. A man reaps what he sows. 8 The one who sows to please his sinful nature, from that nature will reap destruction; the one who sows to please the Spirit, from the Spirit will reap eternal life. 9 Let us not become weary in doing good, for at the proper time we will reap a harvest if we do not give up.

[329] Ps 69:36: The children of his servants will inherit it.

The speaker asked: "Do you know the Scripture verses by heart on healing, prosperity, faith, deliverance? Memorize a dozen of each so you are prepared for every situation that comes to you."[330] Jn. 7:17 says, *"The Father will show you."*

After the talk, Pastor Mich Kealey prayed and said that God's people will come through the furnace without even the smell of smoke if we trust in Him just as it was with the three young men.[331] We are covenant people who can lay claim to the promises of God who cannot lie. God said: *"Yet I will remember the covenant I made with you in the days of your youth, and I will establish an everlasting covenant with you."* [332]

Besides the covenant I have with Almighty God, I also have another covenant with my wife, Jean, who has played a major role in my spiritual growth since we were married. I want to recount a few things spoken into her life that is enriching our ministry as a couple.

On Friday, November 6, 1992, after we heard Chuck Clayton preach, Jean and I went forth for ministry and a word was given by Chuck Clayton and Renee Kealey, the Pastor's wife, for Jean and me.

Chuck said,

---

[330] 1 Pet. 3:15: But in your hearts set apart Christ as Lord. Always be prepared to give an answer to everyone who asks you to give the reason for the hope that you have.

[331] Dan. 3:27

[332] Ez. 16:60; Gen. 9:15 and Lev. 6:42,45

Lord, we bless you for your faithfulness. Lord, we just ask you to bless and minister to your people, speak your words of encouragement and insight. Father, we commit them to your charge and your care. Lord, we ask for a re-stirring, an activation. We thank You for it in Jesus' name. Thank you (He prayed in tongues).

Just what I see in my spirit is like a light covering of dust, and I just hear the Lord saying that another rain is going to come! The Lord said: You've received an early rain some place, that's why I said there's been another early rain! But it has been dry; there's been dust settle over some things, but the Lord says: I'm going to wash it off with the latter rain! He says: I'm going to bring another refreshing rain to you! I'm going to wash away the dust!

He says: I want you to get up! I want you to begin to walk! I want you to begin, even as it was with Abraham; I sent him into the far countries to see what was there, to see what I was going to give him! And He says: I want to open your eyes and allow you to see things you have not seen! I'm not talking about something that is spooky and spiritual or all that, just vision, purpose, destiny, those kinds of things! And He says: I will give you a refreshing! He says: You've gone through that dry period! He says: I'm going to bring a refreshing to you!

He says: And there are even some things in the family you've asked Me about, He says, I've been doing! He says there have been times that you have not been satisfied with it. You've wanted Me to do it one way, but I have to do it another. He says: I want you to have the peace that I'll do you right, saith the Lord! Because if I be for you, who can be against you! So He said: Quit trying to force Me to do it one way, and allow Me to do My way! He said: If you allow Me to work, He said, I will bring it to pass! He said: My way is always the best way! He said: Your vision is good, but it's not complete! He said: My vision is complete! So He said: Don't be concerned about the family, but stand and agree, and continue to resist and fight. And He said: I'll come through for you, even as it was that I remembered My covenant I made with Abraham, I'll remember My covenant I made with you!

So He said: Rise up! And allow Me to wash away the dust! Allow me to give you that refreshing! He said: In doing so, the fresh rain shall bring a new planting! And He said: New fruit shall come forth! New seed shall begin to spring up! So He said: Don't look into the past! But look into the future and you shall surely see My handiwork come to pass!

Then I said: Hallelujia! Praise the Lord!

Then Renee Kealey said to my wife, "What's your name?"

"Jean," she replied.

Renee asked, "Do you travel on the city bus?"

"No," Jean said.

Renee continued,

What I see in my spirit is a bus, and how when you are on a bus you're not real close to people, but you're next to them for a season and then you travel to your destination. And I feel, Jean, that the Lord has placed you as an important life in people, that as you're traveling the Lord will place people that really will not be close attachments, that they will not be people you'll make a long committment to. OK? But the Lord's going to place people for you to encourage them and to exhort and to comfort, that as you are going in, you'll be placed right there, and there will be someone sitting next to you to whom you'll say that word of encouragement. And that you'll have a neat sort of experience.

I felt in my spirit that some people have a mission to Iraq or some people have missions to Great Britain, but I think of you having a mission to strangers; that you are a missionary to strangers. And that as people come into your life, that you're a missionary to them, to minister to them, to give them that personal touch, to give them that encouraging word that you're teaching and that they need, and that you may not see the fruit. But you are ministering to strangers, and the Lord says in the Old Testament that we are to remember what it is like to be strangers, because we are strangers ourselves.

So I feel that the word of the Lord is that you have a calling to strangers: to be prophetic, to step out, to give them a word of encouragement, and to give them a word of exhortation, and to give them comfort, and to smile to them; and just be obedient to the Lord to comfort and encourage the stranger.

Jean received another powerful word through Cindy Orlando on February 19, 1994, at the School of The Holy Spirit in Oak Park, IL, overseen by Burton Seavey.

Cindy said,

Jean, what I saw when I looked at you, what I saw was a glow around your face! And I said: Lord, what is that? He said it was His glow! It was the glow of the Lord! It was the 'glory of God around you.' That is the word I am looking for!

And I just sense that the glory of God just envelopes your life! And I just really felt that He has placed within you a mother's heart! A heart that just reaches out and wraps your arms around people you even don't really know that well, but it just kind of draws them, loves them! And the

Lord says: I had placed those gifts and those qualities within you! And they are precious to Me! They are precious to Me! And I will use them in the days ahead!

I see you ministering to people; just wrapping your arms around them and loving them! There are so many people are out here in the world that have been hurt, that have been wounded, that have been tread down, and I see you coming along side and picking them up, and just holding them close and just loving them. Just, not so much preaching at them, but just loving on them! And as you loved on them, it's the love of God that was getting off on them.

And then that love was going to draw them and heal them. And I saw that He was going to give you a ministry of healing! Of healing the heart! Of healing the wounds that are within people! That you're just going to speak a word, and it may not be to crowds or ten of thousands; it will just be a word here, a word there, as your arms are around somebody, and it may be just a simple "I love you!" or "I care!" or "I'm praying for you!" But those words are going to be His words, and they are going to go deep. They're going to go to the very core where people are hurting. And the Lord is just going to use you as His instrument, to just begin to pour that healing balm of Gilead into people's lives.[333] Because I see that He's going to

---

[333] Jer. 8:22: Is there no balm in Gilead? Is there no physician there? Why then is there no healing for the wound of my people?

work in your life!

And He's already been doing this in you! And I just see it increasing in the days ahead, the ministry of love! That's what I see Him giving you, the ministry of love!

I see your home even open up, people will begin to come to your door, and they're just going to need a place in the weary days ahead! They're going to need just a refuge, a place of shelter! And I see you just providing that! I see you providing a cup of coffee and just a listening ear. And you're just going to be that shelter! And the Lord is going to minister through you!

So don't think, "Who am I? And what do I have to do?" Know that He has a great work for you to do! And that when He takes you home to heaven, I just keep hearing that song over and over in my head about: Thank You! That Ray Bolten sings: Thank You! I just keep hearing, seeing all these people just coming and saying: Thank You! Thank you, for what you did! Thank you for ministering to me. It was you that led me back to the Lord! It was you that healed my broken heart!

And you may not know all that you're going to do, but the Lord knows! And He's just storing those up in heaven and some day you'll hear the Thank You!

CHAPTER 21

Manifesting God's Glory—Virgins Who Are Ready

This is the will of God! Be an instrument of His glory which is manifested in and through your life. Lord, I am pressing on toward the goal—heavenward in Christ Jesus! *"I can do everything through him who gives me strength."* [334] *"For we are God's workmanship, created in Christ Jesus to DO GOOD WORKS, WHICH GOD PREPARED in advance for us to do."* [335]

When one of the intercessors dropped by the office on June 2, 1992, I said: "Wow, do you look bright today; a light is around you; I see angels all around you!" And he shared, "I was taken into the Presence of God through the Lamb of the Passover from about 6 A.M. until after 1 P.M. today."

"The Paschal Lamb in the Old Testament was a type of deliverance, type of His setting His people free. The Lord is taking his people, step by step from cleansing into glorification. We are going to be glorified even in this earth. The Lord showed me: *'Glorify your Son, that your Son may glorify you'* (Jn. 17:1) applies to us too; but how can we glorify God unless He glorifies us and lifts us up to this new higher level of glory that Jesus prayed for at the last supper? In Jn. 17:22, Jesus said: *'I have given them the glory that you gave me, that they may be one as we are one.'* As we inherited the nature of Adam, so we will inherit the nature of Jesus Christ."

---

[334] Phil. 4:13

[335] Eph. 2:10 [Capitalization mine for emphasis]

He encouraged me to read the "Filled in the Fullness" section on page 97 to the end of the chapter in Andrew Murray's book, *In Search of Spiritual Excellence*. He shared a few choice tidbits of revelation, such as, faith is the eyesight of the spirit; if you do not have the concept of what God is telling you, you don't have the kind of faith that makes miracles happen. When God promises someone something, it is accomplished in the spiritual realm, but the time it takes from the Promise to the fulfillment of the Promise in the physical realm depends on where the believer is at and how long it takes that person to get ready, to get himself aligned with God's perfect will.

He said he believes that we are in the last days of spiritual warfare and the enemy is almost defeated, and then the glory of the Lord will come forth through us. He quoted Jn. 1:7, ***"But if we walk in the light as he is in the light, we have fellowship with one another, and the blood of Jesus, His Son, purifies us."*** The converse is also true: If we have not fellowship with Jesus, we walk in darkness.

The parable of the five wise and five foolish virgins demonstrates the importance of being ready and walking in the light. Jesus shared about the five wise and five foolish virgins immediately after He said,

> ***The master of that (wicked) servant will come on a day when he does not expect him and at an hour he is not aware of. He will cut him to pieces and assign him a place with the hypocrites, where there will be weeping and gnashing of teeth. At that time the kingdom of heaven will be like ten virgins who took their lamps and went out to meet***

the bridegroom. Five of them were foolish and five were wise.[336]

Another brother stopped in and I shared about the revelations the Lord had recently been showing me about how we can better worship Him. We must be willing to remove all that is not God from within us so He can take total possession. We must seek deliverance from the spirits of any ancestral or personal sins and any of their manifestations.

First, it is critical that we seek the Lord to show us any hidden claims satan has on us. Identify the specific spirit, such as anger, prostitution, anxiety, pride, deceit, etc. and then profess aloud to another Christian, "In the name of Jesus I repent of those sins and am determined to repudiate and deliver myself of that spirit and any of its many manifestations." In its place we invite Jesus and welcome the fruits of the Holy Spirit. Those demons (spirits) then have no claim on us. As the Lord reveals a spirit that still has a hold or claim on us, we again repudiate that spirit in the name of Jesus.

Remember, it was Jesus who said of the devil: **"The prince of this world is coming. He has no hold on me."** [337] He was saying just as satan has no authority over Him, so, too, he should and can have no hold or authority over us. Then the glory of God will come over us and we will worship Him the way He deserves all our worship.

This brother confessed several strongholds and was delivered of several spirits that still laid claim to him up until now. But no longer! Praise God! You, too, can be delivered of all demon-

---

[336] Mt. 24:50-25:2
[337] Jn. 14:30

ic strangle holds the enemy has on you so the glory of God will manifest itself through your life.

CHAPTER 22

Letter to the Modern Corinthian Church

One day, the Lord put it on my heart that if Paul the apostle were living today, what would God want him to write to the churches of today? His two letters to the Corinthian church were letters of correction and encouragement. So this is what followed. I felt led to include this last section in the book for the benefit of the readers. Not everything in here applies to every church. But generally I believe this is what is on the heart of God today. Please apply to your situation whatever fits, and discard the rest. Discernment is needed to read this chapter. But if there is a point that particularly annoys you, it probably fits your situation and the Lord wants you to deal with it! Be quick to repent!

Beloved of God, I send my greetings to the Modern Corinthian Church with the truth from the Lord Jesus Christ, and my greetings come with a sad heart! O you senseless and childish people! You have been given so much in giftings and callings, but you have been puffed up in pride and arrogance and have operated in such gross carnality! God will not, cannot honor what things man attempts to do or make that can only be done or made by the hands of the Eternally Large and Holy One, God Himself! Repent and fall upon your faces, for I tell you the time is short![338]

Ask the Lord Jesus Christ to send His Spirit to deliver you of all iniquity,[339] so that your blindness will be revealed and

---

[338] Rev. 2:16: 16 Repent; or else I will come unto thee quickly, and will fight against them with the sword of my mouth. [KJV]

[399] Ps. 103:2,3: Bless the LORD, O my soul, and forget not all his benefits: 3 Who forgiveth all thine iniquities; who healeth all thy diseases. [KJV]

healed! Relent and repent! ***"The Kingdom of God is at hand!"*** [340] Empty yourselves and fall humbly on your face before Him, asking Him to take out all iniquity so that the devil will have nothing in you, and have no hold on you! There is a difference between sin and iniquity.[341] Sin can be forgiven, but iniquity will be removed[342] even as your soul prospers![343] Deal with the iniquity inside, the root of sinful actions. Yield yourself; let Jesus have you! When the Lord Jesus Christ rules sovereignly on the inside of you, you will be holy! God will then produce His government on the inside of you, and this will produce righteousness, peace and joy in the Holy Spirit![344]

Though I am not with you in the body, I can see in the spirit that you adults are acting like babies, vying to be the first one to suck on the pacifier, or to crawl into the bassinets, or sleep in the crib! Yes, you claim to be very anointed, but you are fighting over small and unimportant matters! You have been babes in the Lord too long! Signs and wonders are not following you as Jesus indeed promised would follow all true believers![345] Not just pastors or elders, but all true believers![346] Yes, there is much carnal-

---

340 Mt. 3:2

341 Ps. 51:2: Wash away all my iniquity and cleanse me from my sin.

342 Is. 53:5: But he was pierced for our transgressions, he was crushed for our iniquities; the punishment that brought us peace was upon him, and by his wounds we are healed.

343 3 Jn. 2: Beloved, I wish above all things that thou mayest prosper and be in health, even as thy soul prospereth.

344 Rom. 14:17: For the kingdom of God is not meat and drink; but righteousness, and peace, and joy in the Holy Ghost.

345 Mk. 9:23; 10:27

346 Mk. 16:17,18: "And these signs will accompany those who believe: In my name they will drive out demons; they will speak in new tongues; 18 they will pick up snakes with their hands; and when they drink deadly poison, it will not hurt them at all; they will place their hands on sick people, and they will get well."

ity among your leaders! I hear they are jockeying for political position and recognition among themselves! They do not believe that the Giver will make a way for the gift. No one can manipulate God or His people! It is He who will promote you and make a way for your gift.[347][348]

Is it any wonder new Christians will not commit themselves entirely to Jesus when they see adults who claim to be longtime Christians acting so carnally? Where is your witness? Do you not understand that it is the fruit of the Spirit that will make you an effective tool for attracting others to Jesus? Love, joy, peace, patience, kindness, goodness, faithfulness, gentleness and self-control![349] Against such things there is no prohibition! That fruit will draw unbelievers to Jesus like bees to honey! Return to your first love![350]

The gifts of the Spirit are given not as a sign of our holiness, but as essential tools for others, so we can witness to others, heal others, cast out devils, and bring the Kingdom of God from heaven down to earth! Do not grieve the Holy Spirit by denying that He is operating today through the Body of Christ! Jesus the Head has done everything He intended to do on earth! Now He desires to accomplish in these end-times His divine Plan through us, the Body of Christ, and through the Holy Spirit that He sent

---

[347] Ps. 75: 6,7,10: For promotion [cometh] neither from the east, nor from the west, nor from the south. 7 But God [is] the judge: he putteth down one, and setteth up another. 10 All the horns of the wicked also will I cut off; [but] the horns of the righteous shall be exalted. [KJV]

[348] Pr. 18:16: 16 A man's gift maketh room for him, and bringeth him before great men. [KJV]

[349] Gal. 5:22

[350] Rev. 2:5,6: 4 Nevertheless I have [somewhat] against thee, because thou hast left thy first love. 5 Remember therefore from whence thou art fallen, and repent, and do the first works; or else I will come unto thee quickly, and will remove thy candlestick out of his place, except thou repent. [KJV]

upon the earth to be our Helper! It is time for the Body of Jesus on earth to take the kingdom by force.[351]

We are to establish the King's just and righteous rule over a partially unwilling population, and to bring the people of the earth into compliance and obedience to His Kingdom rule for a thousand years in the Millennial Reign of Jesus through His Body, whom we are! How can we expect to rule and reign with Christ when we cannot rule our own bodies, our own minds, our own ambitions!

Many leaders are focusing in on material matters, yes, even compromising on preaching the truth of the gospel to fit the budget! The truth when preached will always upset error but error when preached cannot upset truth. For truth will never contradict itself, for Truth is a Person![352] But He will take away your candlestick![353] *"Jesus said to them, 'I tell you the truth, at the renewal of all things, when the whole earth is born again, when the Son of Man sits on his glorious throne, you who have followed me will also sit on twelve thrones, judging the twelve tribes of Israel.'"*[354] Why are you following after other gods? Putting anything before God is idol worship.[355] That's idol worship to focus on carnal matters.[356]

But avoid foolish controversies and genealogies

---

[351] Mt. 11:12: From the days of John the Baptist until now, the kingdom of heaven has been forcefully advancing, and forceful men lay hold of it.

[352] Jn. 14:6: Jesus answered, "I am the way and the truth and the life.

[353] Rev. 1:5: Remember the height from which you have fallen! Repent and do the things you did at first. If you do not repent, I will come to you and remove your lampstand from its place.

[354] Mt. 19:28

[355] Ex. 20:3, Deut. 5:7 and Mt. 4:10

and arguments and quarrels about the law, because these are unprofitable and useless. Warn a divisive person once, and then warn him a second time. After that, have nothing to do with him. You may be sure that such a man is warped and sinful; he is self-condemned.[357]

When you come together to celebrate communion, the sharing of the Body of Jesus with the Corporate Body of Jesus, recognize Jesus' Body in others, lest you eat and drink condemnation to yourself! Many of you think that if you acknowledge and receive the Sacramental Presence of Jesus, you have fulfilled the commandment: Love God! But I tell you, you can only love God when you love your neighbor! Yes, I tell you, the Body of Christ is both Jesus the Head and Jesus the Body, that is, others in covenant with Jesus! Jesus is the Head of His Bride with whom He identifies Himself intimately! And to be a respecter of persons means that you are not a respecter of God's purpose! Jesus described the Pharisees as respecters of persons when *"He said to them, 'You are the ones who justify yourselves in the eyes of men, but God knows your hearts. What is highly valued among men is detestable in God's sight.'"*[358]

---

[356] 2 Tim. 2:14-19 Keep reminding them of these things. Warn them before God against quarreling about words; it is of no value, and only ruins those who listen. 15 Do your best to present yourself to God as one approved, a workman who does not need to be ashamed and who correctly handles the word of truth. 16 Avoid godless chatter, because those who indulge in it will become more and more ungodly. 17 Their teaching will spread like gangrene.

[357] Tit. 3:9-11

[358] Lk. 16:15

He doesn't care whether you're the best-dressed person in town or a casual dresser.[359] The Lord wants your heart rather than your head or your hands! He wants your obedience rather than your sacrifice![360] God looks at the heart, not the clothes! He sees what is important to Him! The spirit man, not the carnal man! ***"Do not be deceived! God is not mocked,"*** [361] nor can He be deceived, for He is Truth openly made manifest to all who are hungry for truth! Yes, Jesus said: Seek first the Kingdom of heaven and all those others things will be given as a side benefit to those seekers of Him![362]

Get your house in order! Remember that the first shall be last and the last first![363]

I have many things to say to you, but when I come in the flesh I shall deal with them all. For now I shall address those important blatant matters totally out of control and out of God's

---

358 Lk. 16:15

359 Jas. 2:1-5: My brothers, as believers in our glorious Lord Jesus Christ, don't show favoritism. 2 Suppose a man comes into your meeting wearing a gold ring and fine clothes, and a poor man in shabby clothes also comes in. 3 If you show special attention to the man wearing fine clothes and say, "Here's a good seat for you," but say to the poor man, "You stand there" or "Sit on the floor by my feet," 4 have you not discriminated among yourselves and become judges with evil thoughts? 5 Listen, my dear brothers: Has not God chosen those who are poor in the eyes of the world to be rich in faith and to inherit the kingdom he promised those who love him.

360 1 Sam. 15:22,23: But Samuel replied: "Does the LORD delight in burnt offerings and sacrifices as much as in obeying the voice of the LORD? To obey is better than sacrifice, and to heed is better than the fat of rams. 23 For rebellion is like the sin of divination, and arrogance like the evil of idolatry.

361 Gal. 6:7

362 Mt. 6:33: But seek first his kingdom and his righteousness, and all these things will be given to you as well.

363 Mt. 20:16: "So the last will be first, and the first will be last."

order![364]

Look in the word of God! Seek the Scriptures, which were written for our instruction![365] [366] And remember His Kingdom shall confirm His covenant with His people. We are a covenant people,[367] yes, we are a corporate Body joined together in unity so that God can command the blessings![368] If we are not in covenant with those He has put in our midst, He shall command the curses. Remember, Achan put the covenant people in the way of God's wrath![369] Achan brought the wrath of God upon the whole camp and the whole army of God was defeated overwhelmingly by a small army of the enemy. The evil one had a hold on the entire corporate body, which was infected and affected with defeat. For Achan's sin was not only one of greed, fear and distrust that God could not provide for his needs, but his sin was one of idolatry. Achan stole and hid away the Babylonian garment which represented the power of a Babylonian cultic priest whose power he coveted. The occultic practices place magical power in things, in articles and perverted concoctions and potions dedicated to the evil one. His was a desire to usurp authority through magic and

---

[364] 2 Cor. 13:10: This is why I write these things when I am absent, that when I come I may not have to be harsh in my use of authority--the authority the Lord gave me for building you up, not for tearing you down.

[365] Jn. 5:39: Search the scriptures; for in them ye think ye have eternal life: and they are they which testify of me. [KJV]

[366] Mt. 22:29: Jesus replied, "You are in error because you do not know the Scriptures or the power of God.

[367] Ex. 19:5,6: Now therefore, if ye will obey my voice indeed, and keep my covenant, then ye shall be a peculiar treasure unto me above all people: for all the earth [is] mine: 6 And ye shall be unto me a kingdom of priests, and an holy nation. [KJV]

[368] Ps. 133:1,3: How good and pleasant it is when brothers live together in unity! 3 It is as if the dew of Hermon were falling on Mount Zion. For there the LORD bestows his blessing, even life forevermore.

[369] Josh. 7:1-26

witchcraft. Achan's sin was reflective of the covetness of Korah who had rebelled and desired to be in Moses' position of power and authority by whatever means necessary.[370] God dealt swiftly and decisively with that covenant-breaking sin.

Be released, in the name of Jesus! Repudiate everything in you that is not of God! Close the doors and windows of your body to the enemy! And open the doors and windows to Jesus who will open you a window from heaven and pour out such blessings you will not be able to contain it all.[371] Pray for an open heaven, and the Sovereign Lord God who hears the prayers of the just shall hear your request.[372]

Spend time with the Lord, for He wants to become intimate with His Bride-to-be![373] And know that we have at our disposal everything we need to defeat the enemy! Get ready to rule and reign with Christ! For though we have a free will, the Holy Spirit is such a gentleman that He will never overrule our will!

Surrender your will to Him and give Him permission to root out all those deep roots of iniquity that remain within you even after you have repented and been forgiven of all your sins! The blood of Jesus blots out all sins, but only the grace of God, received freely, gradually and progressively as we continue to repent and are able to receive deliverance, can peel off the layers

---

[370] Num. 16:1-40 and Jude 11

[371] Mal. 3:10

[372] Ps. 50:23: "He who sacrifices thank offerings honors me, and he prepares the way so that I may show him the salvation of God."

[373] S of S: 1:2-4: 2 Let him kiss me with the kisses of his mouth: for thy love [is] better than wine. 3 Because of the savour of thy good ointments thy name [is as] ointment poured forth, therefore do the virgins love thee. 4 Draw me, we will run after thee: the king hath brought me into his chambers: we will be glad and rejoice in thee, we will remember thy love more than wine: the upright love thee. [KJV]

of iniquity that remain behind, and heal the scars. God expects us to be holy even as He is holy![374] And what He expects and commands us to do and be, that He is able to accomplish with our cooperation and willingness to receive freely His gifts!

When you pray, acknowledge first His Sovereignty over heaven and earth! Call to remembrance who He is, and acknowledge His Majestic Presence, not for His sake, but for your sake! For when you are praying, it is the Sovereignty of God that brings your prayers to the altar of God with purity under the Blood of Jesus![375] Plead the blood of Jesus upon your prayers.[376][377]

Many of you do not praise God's Sovereignty! Instead you pray your petition of wants! And God says, "Put Me in remembrance of My word so I can move on your behalf!" Not so God knows it, but so you know it! What you do is contrary to what God says: You shall have no other god before Me! When you bring your petitions before Him without recognizing His

---

[374] Ex. 22:31; Lev. 11:44,45, 19:2; 20:7,26; Deut. 7:6, 14:2, 26:19; Is. 62:12; 1 Cor. 1:2; Eph. 1:4

[375] Rev. 7:3,4: Another angel, who had a golden censer, came and stood at the altar. He was given much incense to offer, with the prayers of all the saints, on the golden altar before the throne. 4 The smoke of the incense, together with the prayers of the saints, went up before God from the angel's hand.

[376] Rom. 3:24: Being justified freely by his grace through the redemption that is in Christ Jesus: 25 Whom God hath set forth [to be] a propitiation through faith in his blood, to declare his righteousness for the remission of sins that are past, through the forbearance of God; 26 To declare, [I say], at this time his righteousness: that he might be just, and the justifier of him which believeth in Jesus.

[377] Col. 1:19-22: 19 For God was pleased to have all his fullness dwell in him, 20 and through him to reconcile to himself all things, whether things on earth or things in heaven, by making peace through his blood, shed on the cross. 21 Once you were alienated from God and were enemies in your minds because of your evil behavior. 22 But now he has reconciled you by Christ's physical body through death to present you holy in his sight, without blemish and free from accusation.

Sovereignty and His perfect Will, you first bring all your gods that are your idols before Him! This is what you are saying: "I am going to come to communion today, God! But here's all my little gods, and they're all lined up here! Take care of them! My motor boat won't run today! My car's got a flat tire! My TV needs fixing! My washer and my dryer are broken! Change my spouse!" And you have never even declared who He is! All these little gods are lined up there, but where is God?

God says, "What is this?" So out of His mercy and grace He sent Someone to help you by teaching you to pray properly![378] Why not just declare who He is, and say, "God, I do need some help! I acknowledge that You are my Source! You are My Helper! Change me! You are Sovereign and Almighty! I praise You and worship You above all! You are All Holy!"[379] See, Jesus is concerned about every need you have! But it grieves the Holy Spirit for you to bring petitions amiss to Him! Because if you seek first the kingdom of God, all these things will be added to you![380] And you don't have to go around grieving God![381]

Instead you can pray like Daniel did and get rapid response from the Lord. God has His proper order even in bringing our

---

[378] Mt. 6:9: "This, then, is how you should pray: "'Our Father in heaven, hallowed be your name, 10 your kingdom come, your will be done on earth as it is in heaven. 11 Give us today our daily bread. 12 Forgive us our debts, as we also have forgiven our debtors. 13 And lead us not into temptation, but deliver us from the evil one.

[379] 1 Tim. 1:17: Now to the King eternal, immortal, invisible, the only God, be honor and glory for ever and ever. Amen.

[380] Mt. 6:33,34: But seek ye first the kingdom of God, and his righteousness; and all these things shall be added unto you. 34 Take therefore no thought for the morrow: for the morrow shall take thought for the things of itself. Sufficient unto the day [is] the evil thereof.

[381] Ps. 50:23: Whoso offereth praise glorifieth me: and to him that ordereth [his] conversation [aright] will I shew the salvation of God. [KJV]

petitions to Him. Daniel recognized God's Sovereignty:

> *Daniel answered and said, Blessed be the name of God for ever and ever: for wisdom and might are his: And he changeth the times and the seasons: he removeth kings, and setteth up kings: he giveth wisdom unto the wise, and knowledge to them that know understanding: He revealeth the deep and secret things: he knoweth what [is] in the darkness, and the light dwelleth with him. I thank thee, and praise thee, O thou, God of my fathers, who hast given me wisdom and might, and hast made known unto me now what we desired of thee.* "[382]

Like the disciples, you can ask Jesus: *"Lord, teach us how to pray!"*[383] *"Offer unto God thanksgiving; and pay thy vows unto the most High: And call upon me in the day of trouble: I will deliver thee, and thou shalt glorify me."*[384]

It is the inspired word of God which we confess and profess that angels listen for. These ministering spirits operate on our behalf, but they only listen to the word of God, whether that word of God comes from the Throne in heaven or from the Throne on earth [God within us]. Once spoken, the ministering angels rush to execute these words of God.[385]

---

[382] Dan. 2:20-23

[383] Lk. 11:1

[384] Ps. 50:14,15: Offer unto God thanksgiving; and pay thy vows unto the most High: 15 And call upon me in the day of trouble: I will deliver thee, and thou shalt glorify me. [KJV]

[385] Heb. 1:14: Are they not all ministering spirits, sent forth to minister for them who shall be heirs of salvation?

I hear some of you are robbing God![386] Don't you know that bank robbers are severely judged, especially when they rob from the Possessor of heaven and earth? Where do you think you can hide from this Judge? All tithes, the first-fruits, and offerings belong to God! If you rob from God, He will see to it that the devourer has an open door to take more than you robbed from God! Close that door to the enemy by honoring God with the first 10% of everything you receive! Remember that the income from your job is not your source of money! God is your source! Your job is nothing more than the opportunity to obtain seed money so that by planting that seed, you shall have a great harvest! What you sow, you shall reap![387] That's a Kingdom Principle! And God stands by His word! His word is truth itself, for God cannot lie![388] He is holy! ***"God is not a man, that he should lie, nor a son of man, that he should change his mind. Does he speak and then not act? Does he promise and not fulfill?"*** [389]

Do not feign revival by trying to play God and thereby

---

386 Mal. 3:8-12: Will a man rob God? Yet ye have robbed me. But ye say, Wherein have we robbed thee? In tithes and offerings. 9 Ye [are] cursed with a curse: for ye have robbed me, [even] this whole nation. 10 Bring ye all the tithes into the storehouse, that there may be meat in mine house, and prove me now herewith, saith the LORD of hosts, if I will not open you the windows of heaven, and pour you out a blessing, that [there shall] not [be room] enough [to receive it]. {pour...: Heb. empty out} 11 And I will rebuke the devourer for your sakes, and he shall not destroy the fruits of your ground; neither shall your vine cast her fruit before the time in the field, saith the LORD of hosts. {destroy: Heb. corrupt} 12 And all nations shall call you blessed: for ye shall be a delightsome land, saith the LORD of hosts.

387 Gal. 6:7

388 Is. 5:16: 20 Woe unto them that call evil good, and good evil; that put darkness for light, and light for darkness; that put bitter for sweet, and sweet for bitter!

389 Num. 23:19

attempt to do what only a Sovereign God can do! Fakers do not fool God! He knows your heart! God says revival will come sovereignly *"if my people, who are called by my name, will humble themselves and pray and seek my face and turn from their wicked ways, then will I hear from heaven and will forgive their sin and will heal their land."*[390] So humble yourselves, pray and seek His face, and turn and repent from your wicked ways! Stop organizing carnal crusades and calling them "Revival!" *"I would rather have you hot or cold, but lukewarmness will I vomit out of My mouth!"*[391] God is saying, "I hate mediocrity!"

And when you come together to worship and to minister by the Holy Spirit to one another, thereby imparting what God has imparted to you,[392] do not fake being slain in the Spirit to oblige the person ministering.[393] That is out of order! When the Spirit slays and moves sovereignly, all will know His Holy Spirit is present by the signs and wonders following His true ministers, those He has sent. The Lord says, "My sent ones will always operate in My power by My Spirit, and not operate in carnal techniques of persuasion, manipulation and trickery."

Do you know what Covenant is? Do you know that covenant is a total exchange? Covenant is giving everything you have in exchange for what He has to give![394] What an exchange!

---

390 2 Chr. 7:14

391 Rev. 3:15,16

392 Rom. 1:11,12: I long to see you so that I may impart to you some spiritual gift to make you strong-- 12 that is, that you and I may be mutually encouraged by each other's faith.

393 Some people that are not truly slain in the Spirit, fall down as a swoon gesture to oblige the minister. This does not impress the Lord in the least.

God says, in effect, *"My lover is mine and I am his . . . I am my lover's and my lover is mine."*[395] Did you not enter into covenant with your God and with one another? Did you not:

1) Hear from God that your pastor is to be the shepherd of your soul and therefore submit to him as your appointed and anointed shepherd under the Chief Shepherd?

2) Agree to give tithes, offerings and alms through the fellowship in which I have placed you to be a part of?

3) Agree to be committed, to be involved, to come assembled ready to worship, to participate and to share with one another as a team?

4) Submit yourselves to be teachable?

Recognize God's sent ones, those in the five-fold ministry of apostle, prophet, evangelist, pastor and teacher. For upon these offices the Lord has placed His power and authority to bind and loose and to rule and reign in His domain. We are called to be priests and kings![396] But we must become perfected as saints of God! This is why He gave us the apostle, prophet, pastor, teacher and evangelist![397] God has His order! Submit to God's order and quit boxing with God![398] Your arm is too short to box with God!

---

[394] See Gen. chap. 15 and 17 wherein the Lord entered into blood covenant with Abram, exchanging everything including protection of each other, names, etc. For more information on blood covenant exchange, see the audio tape, *Blood Covenant,* Gold Spirit Ministries, 2627 N. 114th St., Milwaukee, WI 53226.

[395] S of S. 2:16; 6:3

[396] Rev. 1:6 and 5:10

[397] Eph. 4:11-15: 1 And he gave some, apostles; and some, prophets; and some, evangelists; and some, pastors and teachers; 12 For the perfecting of the saints, for the work of the ministry, for the edifying of the body of Christ: 13 Till all come in the unity of the faith, and of the knowledge of the Son of God, unto a perfect man, unto the measure of the stature of the fulness of Christ: {in: or, into} {stature: or, age} 14 That we [henceforth] be no more children, tossed to

His arm is not too short![399] It is not a fair match and you will lose the fight! Submit!

No eclectic choosing and rejecting of truth [A Burger King® mentality: "Have it YOUR way."™] is allowed in the kingdom of God. Someone said: There is your way and my way and Yahweh! Deal with the monster of pride—the macho man and the fairy tale female. God detests pride, but loves the humble! Yes, God resists the proud, but gives grace and favor to the humble of heart![400] Become lovable by submitting your will and your way to that of Yahweh! He is the Way, the Truth and the Life! His way leads to truth which gives life!

A Burger King® mentality says: I will believe this word of God as true, but I reject this word of God because it doesn't fit in with my theology and the way I was taught![401] And I'm too comfortable to change my ways! I'll have it MY WAY! And I'll continue to play the fool! Who do you think you are? Who do you think God is? Is there any comparison between you and God when you are outside of His will?[402] Compare light with utter darkness![403] O foolish man! Repent and humble yourself! Seek

---

and fro, and carried about with every wind of doctrine, by the sleight of men, [and] cunning craftiness, whereby they lie in wait to deceive; 15 But speaking the truth in love, may grow up into him in all things, which is the head, [even] Christ:

[398] 2 Chr. 13:12

[399] Num. 11:23: The LORD answered Moses, "Is the LORD's arm too short? You will now see whether or not what I say will come true for you."

[400] Pr. 3:34; Ps. 138:6; 1 Pet. 5:5

[401] 1 Thes. 4:7: 8 Therefore, he who rejects this instruction does not reject man but God, who gives you his Holy Spirit.

[402] Rom. 9:20,21: But who are you, O man, to talk back to God? "Shall what is formed say to him who formed it, 'Why did you make me like this?'" 21 Does not the potter have the right to make out of the same lump of clay some pottery for noble purposes and some for common use?

God while He can still be found![404]

Our enemies are not flesh and blood, but the spirit-demons that control flesh and blood. If we do not recognize that our battle is not against flesh and blood, but against the principalities and powers that control people, we will lose.[405] For when we war in the flesh against flesh that is controlled by the spirit-demons, we will always lose the battle. We cannot fight spirits with fleshly ammunition; we need spiritual ammunition, called spiritual warfare weapons.

Our biggest battles will be fought in gaining victory over ourselves. We must be delivered of all iniquity within us that remains as the residue of sins for which we have already repented.[406] As an example, if we have repented for anger or lust, but we are still tempted with impatience or lustful thoughts, this is the iniquity that remains. We must ask the Lord to deliver us of this so we can allow the presence of God within us to become manifested in our lives, even so others can see this transformation and give glory to God.

The way to victory over the iniquity within is death to self, death on the cross with Jesus![407] ***"For to me, to live is Christ and to die is gain."*** [408] A dead man cannot be offended by what

---

[403] Job 12: 25 They grope in darkness with no light.

[404] Deut. 4:29, Ez. 8:21-23, Hos. 3:5 and Acts 17:26

[405] 2 Cor. 10:3-5: For though we walk in the flesh, we do not war after the flesh:

[406] (For the weapons of our warfare [are] not carnal, but mighty through God to the pulling down of strong holds;) 5 Casting down imaginations, and every high thing that exalteth itself against the knowledge of God, and bringing into captivity every thought to the obedience of Christ.

406 2 Tim. 2:21: If a man therefore purge himself from these, he shall be a vessel unto honour, sanctified, and meet for the master's use, [and] prepared unto every good work.

you say about him, nor will he react even if you hit him and kick him as hard as you can! Dead men cannot suffer! Dead men don't fight back! Are you fighting back, or are you dead to self? God will let you know when He tests you in those areas in which you need to die! ***"My grace is sufficient for you!"*** [409] Press on to the goal to win the prize for which God has called us heavenward in Christ Jesus. [410] Live by the Spirit, and you will not gratify the desires of the sinful nature. [411]

Pray that when I come to you in the flesh, I will be able to bring strong meat for you to eat! [412] Receive these words with an open, humble spirit, for they will reward you with covenant blessings that the Anointed One has promised to those who are His!

Greetings in the Lord Jesus Christ who has come in the flesh to sanctify our spirit, soul and body and to destroy any anti-

---

[407] Gal. 2:20,21: I have been crucified with Christ and I no longer live, but Christ lives in me. The life I live in the body, I live by faith in the Son of God, who loved me and gave himself for me. 21 I do not set aside the grace of God, for if righteousness could be gained through the law, Christ died for nothing! Phil. 3:10,11: I want to know Christ and the power of his resurrection and the fellowship of sharing in his sufferings, becoming like him in his death, 11 and so, somehow, to attain to the resurrection from the dead.

[408] Phil. 1:21: For to me, to live is Christ and to die is gain.

[409] 2 Cor. 12:9

[410] Phil. 3:14: I press on toward the goal to win the prize for which God has called me heavenward in Christ Jesus.

[411] Gal. 5:16

[412] 2 Cor. 13:10,11: This is why I write these things when I am absent, that when I come I may not have to be harsh in my use of authority--the authority the Lord gave me for building you up, not for tearing you down. 11 Finally, brothers, good-by. Aim for perfection, listen to my appeal, be of one mind, live in peace. And the God of love and peace will be with you.

christ spirit[413][414] that still remains in us. Amen.

[413] Rom. 16:20: The God of peace will soon crush Satan under your feet.

[414] 1 Jn. 3:8: He who does what is sinful is of the devil, because the devil has been sinning from the beginning. The reason the Son of God appeared was to destroy the devil's work.

Conclusion

In conclusion to *The Testimony of Jesus – Book 1,* let me say that the Lord's hand has been on me strongly just as He desires to strongly put His hand upon your life, dear reader.

I have made many mistakes, but through all of this the Lord has taught me humility and has purged me of much iniquity. One of the greatest mistakes I have made is not praying over and discerning which people the Lord wanted me to be associated with to accomplish God's perfect will. Another mistake is not hearing clearly the voice of the Lord and moving out ahead of Him in presumption, thinking I was doing His will. His timing is critical to doing His will on earth!

But the journey goes on and we all are learning. We cannot get away with what we used to be able to get away with. The fiery furnace gets warmer as He desires to purge out all iniquity so His Glory can shine through us to others as He desires. He wants to inhabit our entire house, not be relegated to the closet. Then we can hear and see plainly only what the Father is saying and doing. We continue to praise the Lord in every circumstance and *"swell with joy"!* [415]

Although this concludes *The Testimony Of Jesus: The Spirit Of Prophecy - Book 1, as spoken to one of His servant scribes,* the Lord willing, other volumes shall come forth. The Lord shall lead. *"To man belong the plans of the heart, but from the Lord comes the reply of the tongue." "Commit to the Lord whatever you do, and your plans will succeed." "When a man's ways are pleasing to the*

---

[415] Is. 60:5

Lord, he makes even his enemies live at peace with him." "In his heart a man plans his course, but the Lord determines his steps." "Many are the plans in a man's heart, but it is the Lord's purpose that prevails." [416]

So I continue seeking to hear only the Lord's voice and to see only what the Father does. Then I will fulfill His perfect will for my calling from the Lord in all wisdom! Lord, I seek You! Show me the way! Take me out of the wilderness when You are ready! Amen!

I return to Pr. 3:5,6 which has helped me stay the course through thick and thin: *"Trust in the Lord with all your heart and lean not on your own understanding; in all your ways acknowledge him, and he will make your paths straight."*

---

[416] Pr. 16:1,3,7,9; 19:21

EPILOGUE[417]

There is a compelling reason why I wrote this book at this time! The Lord spoke directly and often over a few months through His prophets to unmistakendly get the message into my spirit to write it now! Read the words of His prophets!

On August 16, 1998, a prophetic word through Larry Bishop prompted me to publish this as soon as possible, the first of several books to come:

I'm going to give you a ministry, a ministry that the endtime people[418] will recognize straight from God! Because it will be coming out of the River of Life and from Me! So, what you're going to feel in the next few months is a stretching process! And you're going to have to leave things that you've been doing that you don't want to leave! You're going to have to stretch out of things that you don't want to, that you just don't want to leave! And God says: "Trust Me! Trust Me because I'm stretching you out!" And what He's going to do is bring you right back to the same point to bring amplification to everything that you love! You're not giving it up! He's just making a broader area for it to grow, everything that's in you! God says:

---

[417] Most prophetic words have been preserved as spoken and not corrected for grammar, etc., to preserve the accuracy of the prophetic message and meaning.

[418] Endtime people are those referred to by Jesus as people living after Him. No one knows when the end shall come, but we can know the season. Let him hear who has ears to hear. "But, beloved, be not ignorant of this one thing, that one day [is] with the Lord as a thousand years, and a thousand years as one day." (2 Pet. 3:8)

"Forget the past! Put that behind you and do what I tell you to do now, because the time is so short! The harvest is so great." But He says: "I'm going to make you a wide area in My Body to work in!" Now, I don't know anything about you, but you have books in you! You have a writing ability! And if you will put some of those things that God has put in you down, then God will bless you with finances! Does that make sense to you?

I responded: I've been praying about a timing for that because I do a lot of writing! And there's a lot that could be written and published, but I don't have the timing yet. Larry said,

Well, this is the time! And that's some of that stretching, you know! That's some of that stretching, and He put that in a kind of like a river form so that you'd know. But I see you, you feel like, man, I don't have time to do this; I don't have time to do that! But if you will collate what God has already given you, the Body needs it now! And that's going to bring you a substance that you haven't had in the past. It's also going to finance your ministry, parts of it! Also it's going to give you the ability to give to ministries God designates! Every time He makes a channel, He also makes a way for you to funnel; He funnels through you! He funnels through you! Well, you just got so much in you that it's been there, it's been there, and He's saving it for this time! This is the time! This is the time!

I expect this book to go to many nations and to be translated into many languages in fulfillment of several prophetic words spoken over my wife and me. The following was spoken through a minister who operates powerfully in the prophetic, Pastor Owen Johnson, at the Prophetic Presbytery For Spiritual Leaders held in Milwaukee, Wisconsin on November 22, 1997. Owen had this word for my wife and me:

The Lord says that you two are very, very important to the kingdom! And the things that you do don't seem to be significant, but the Lord says, The things that you do are very significant! And the Lord has thee in place, and He shall order thee, yeah, even into fresh things, even new things! For the Lord is very, not impressed, but very pleased with your sincerity and your commitment to God, for it's from the heart! And it has feeling, and God even feels the feeling of your heart! And the Lord saith that even the little things that you do for the brethren are not without recognition, for the Lord is laying even the blessing up in store for thee! And the Lord saith: This isn't going to come to a quick conclusion or a short end concerning your life, because He's going to work in your bodies, yeah, even to increase you! Yeah, even lengthen your days, for longevity shall increase!

Then looking directly at me and directing this to me, Owen continued,

And even that which afflicted thee in times past [419] *is long since gone over the horizon! It shall not latch back into thine body! For, yeah, the Lord's blessing is upon thee to enrich thee! And, yeah, even stand as one who encourages, one who moves by the influence of the Spirit in revelation! And, yeah, the Lord shall bless many people through that which you record, that which you do on the typewriter, or the computer, whatever it is, but I see you doing this* [He gestured typing with his fingers]. *For, yeah, even your material which seems to be so insignificant, shall even travel this globe, and even people shall be blessed through that that you record, that that you reproduce, saith the Lord, not only in printed material, but also in cassette!*

Another word was spoken at the Thanksgiving Prayer Breakfast for Intercessors held in Milwaukee, WI, on November 21, 1998, through Dr. Mildred C. Harris of God First Ministries of Chicago. Dr. Harris approached me while singing, *"God's will shall be done on the earth! God's will shall be done on the earth! As it is in heaven, so shall it be on earth!"* She took and held my right hand with her right hand, and prophetically sang,

Man of God! Man of God, I see! Take what you need, you see! What you need, from Jesus! Take what you need! Receive what you will from Jesus! Don't worry about the work, you see!

---

[419] I was miraculously healed of cancer which had spread to the lymph nodes on September 17, 1991.

God's going to let you complete the work, you see! Oh, yes, it's not about your age, you see! God says: "You're right on time," you see! He had to take you the way He did to give you wisdom and knowledge, you see, for the people that are waiting! And there are people waiting, you see, that need your knowledge of your God, you see! Oh, He's taking you into a new place now—in God, you see! So don't question what is happening to you. Just know that in the heavenly atmosphere, in Him, that He's doing a new thing in thee! Let Him do it! Let Him do it! Let Him do it! Oh, yes! Oh, He's raining on your crops, you see! Where there was a drought, but now, you see, looking up into the heavens, I see, like a palm in the heavens, like a cloud![420] Aha! Rain on your crops! Rain on the things you planted, oh, yes, you see! Oh, many years ago you thought that it was just, oh, well, so-so! Aha! But God says: "I've not forgotten your faithfulness," you see! Yes, there are times you became so discouraged, I see! Aha! Lord, what about me here? Am I doing right, Lord? Reveal it to me, Lord! O God, I just want to do this for you, Lord, before I go home, Lord God! But He says: "I've heard your prayers." "Yes, and every seed that you've sown in the earth," God says, "It shall grow! Reaping time! Harvest time! Reaping time! Harvest time! Reaping time! Harvest time!" Oh, yeh, you got

---

[420] 1 Kgs. 18:44: The seventh time the servant reported, "A cloud as small as a man's hand is rising from the sea." So Elijah said, "Go and tell Ahab, 'Hitch up your chariot and go down before the rain stops you.'"

more down in your belly, you see, yeh, to be released on the earth, you see! Oh, yeh, you got wisdom and knowledge, and you're a well-seasoned man of God, I see! But He's going to take you into spiritual realms, so let go and let God have His way! And know that it is God, I say! Know it's God, just like when John was taken up in the spirit! Aha! Yes, He's going to take you up! He's going to take you up and have some new experiences, I say! Another dimension! Another dimension for your ministry! A newer dimension, so write all these things, I say! Continue to write and study, yes, but write, I say, for there shall be many that shall read thy writings, I say! Um-huh! God has blessed you greatly, man of God, I say! And many don't know who you are, I say! But you are a great priest in the kingdom, I say! Promotion! Promotion, I say! Jesus says: "Promotion today!" You've graduated, I see! Aha! He puts a scroll in your hands, I see! Yeh, now take the pen and paper and write! In Jesus' name! In Jesus' name! In Jesus' name! In Jesus' name! In Jesus' name! In Jesus' name! In Jesus' name!

Other precise and strong words of encouragement urging me to write this book at this time came in December of 1998 and January, 1999.

Owen Johnson prophesied on December 17, 1998:

Brother Vern, you and your wife, come! Glory to

God! Hallelujah! Thank You, Lord! When I was seeking the Lord about both of you today, He showed me your background that you came from a staunch Catholic background. I know that you were a priest and you were a nun. And the Lord didn't necessarily bring you out of that completely to the degree . . . He's going use you among the Catholics. I mean, He showed that to me very, very clearly, that you're going to have a profound effect witnessing to Catholic people! And the Lord showed me that you're going to be putting a book together about your life and about your testimony of healing, and that that testimony of healing is going to be instrumental in touching a lot of Catholic hearts, not just Catholic people, but a lot of other people as well. For God has placed you in the position that you're in, and His arms of love just surround your family . . . And the Lord says that because of your faithfulness to help in your giving and also helping other ministers, the Lord is going to reward you in these last days like you've never dreamed of! Because He's going to even wake you up in the middle of the night and show you what you are to do about investments and how you are to shift things around, and how you are to do things!

For the Lord says that you are going to receive the reward of a prophet! And one of the rewards of the prophet goes like this: The man and the woman who ministered to the prophet, (2 Kgs. 4:8-37, 8:1-6) *who built the little room there and took care of the prophet, before the famine came, the prophet went to them and told them that it was coming. And he warned them and told them to go into another land to be sustained. And when they came back, their property was confiscated. And guess what? God gave back, moved on the king, made the king give their property back. And everything that was planted on that land the whole time they were gone had to be returned to them too. So God says that the reward of a prophet is going to flow to you both!*

And you're going to put more than one book or pamphlet together. And the Lord wants you to think about what He's saying to you tonight, because He really wants to bless some Catholic people. And Catholic people will be more apt to listen to Catholic people or people that come from a Catholic tradition than they would a Protestant. But you're going to testify about the in-filling of the Holy Ghost! You're going to testify about healing and deliverance! And testify about how you were a priest and how you were a nun, and how God brought all this together! And God's going to really use it among Catholic people, saith the Lord. And Protestants too! I'll just carry that on my book table, the Lord willing. Amen! God bless you!

I said, "Bless you. Amen! Bless you! Thank you. Hallelujah!"

Owen asked, *"Have you ever thought of putting that in a book?"*

I said, "Yes, I'm working on it!" Owen responded, *"Oh, glory!* [Laughter] *Isn't that something! Go into greater detail, not just . . . don't just emphasize the healing of the cancer; go into greater details, I mean, leading up to that, because that would be very interesting reading."*

Wayman Thomas on December 31, 1998, was ministering, saying, *"A shift in the Spirit! Receive it, saith the Spirit of the Lord!"* Then touching me on the forehead he said,

Bless this man of God! Bless! Bless, bless, bless this man of God! Write! Write! Write! Write! Write! Write! Write! Write! The Spirit says: Write! Write! Write! Write! Books! Books! Books! Magazines! Write! Write! Write! Father, bless! Bless! Bless!

Pastor Bill Alston on January 16, 1999, said in a prophetic prayer over me, *"We thank You, God, that he's going to be a help to Your Body! He's going to be a help right now, God, publicizing who You are!"*

And finally Jan Calvin that same day said,

I heard the Father who said that you're going to be writing books! I could see you as a person that has a draw. You keep books; you write! You do a lot of writing! He said: You're going to also write books and the books that you're going to write,

they're going to help others! And the other peo-
ple that are going to be walking, that are going to
be walking with you, He said: Share your books!
Share your wisdom! And share your thoughts!

I pray you enjoyed this first volume of *The Testimony of Jesus!* If you did, please share it with others! God bless you!

Appendix A: Articles of Faith Taken From The Kingdom of Heaven Christian Ministries

The fundamental teachings of Jesus' Church are reflected in the following clear statements of faith:

1.   We believe in the plenary-verbal inspiration of the accepted canon of Scriptures as originally given. The Scriptures are infallible, inerrant, and the sole and final authority for all matters of faith and conduct (II Timothy 3:16; I Corinthians 2:13).

2.   We believe in the Eternal Godhead who has revealed Himself as One God existing in Three Persons, Father, Son and Holy Spirit, distinguishable but indivisible (Matthew 28:19; II Corinthians 13:14).

3.   We believe in the creation, test and fall of man as recorded in Genesis; his total spiritual depravity and inability to attain to Divine righteousness (Romans 5:12,18).

4.   We believe in the Lord Jesus Christ, the Saviour of men, conceived of the Holy Spirit, born of the Virgin Mary, very God and very Man (Luke 1:26-35; John 1:14-18; Isaiah 7:14; 9:6).

5.   We believe Christ died for our sins, was buried and rose again the third day, and personally appeared to His disciples (I Corinthians 15:1-4; Romans 4:25).

6.   We believe in the bodily ascension of Jesus into heaven, His exaltation and personal, literal and bodily coming again the second time for His Church (John 14:2,3; I Thessalonians 4:13-18).

7. We believe in the salvation of sinners by grace, through repentance and faith in the perfect and sufficient work of the cross of Calvary by which we obtain remission of sins (Ephesians 2:8,9; Hebrews 9:12,22; Romans 5:11).

8. We believe in the necessity of water baptism by immersion in the Name of the Eternal Godhead in order to fulfill the command of the Lord Jesus Christ (Matthew 28:19; Acts 2:34-36; 19:1-6).

9. We believe in the baptism of the Holy Spirit as a real experience at or subsequent to salvation, with the Scriptural evidence, namely, speaking in other tongues as the Spirit gives utterance (Acts 2:1-4; 8:14-17; 10:44-46; Galatians 3:14-15).

10. We believe in the operation of the Gifts of the Spirit as enumerated in I Corinthians 12, 13, 14, as manifested in the Early Church.

11. We believe in the Spirit-filled life, a life of separation from worldly values and perfecting of holiness in the fear of God as expressing the true Christian faith (Ephesians 5:18; II Corinthians 6:14; 7:1; Gal. 5:16).

12. We believe in the healing of the body by Divine power, or Divine healing in its varied aspects as practiced in the Early Church (Acts 4:30; Romans 8:11; I Corinthians 12:9; James 5:14).

13. We believe in the table of the Lord, commonly called the Communion or the Lord's Supper, for believers (I Corinthians 11:28-32; Matthew 26:26-28).

14. We believe in the reality and personality of the Devil and eternal judgment in the Lake of Fire for the Devil and his angels (Matthew 25:41; Revelation 20:14,15).

15. We believe in eternal life for believers (John 5:24; 3:16), and eternal punishment for the unbelievers (Mark 9:43-48; II Thessalonians 1:9; Revelation 20:10-15).

16. We believe that there is one true universal Church, made up of genuine believers, but this one universal Church is also composed of many local Churches in given localities. These Churches are under the sovereign Headship of the Lord Jesus Christ, exercising autonomous government under Him, administering all its local affairs and ministry, as well as the propagation of the Gospel (Acts 15:22; with Matthew 16:18; 18:15-20).

17. We believe that Government is ordained of God, and the powers that be are ordained as ministers of God to us for good. To resist the powers and the ordinances is to resist the ordinance of God. We are subject not only for wrath sake but for conscience sake, rendering to all their dues, custom to whom custom, fear to whom fear, honor to whom honor. We declare our loyalty to our Government and its leaders and will assist in every way possible consistent with our faith in the Scriptures as Christian citizens (Romans 13).

> We believe it was Jesus Christ who gave some to be apostles; and some, prophets; and some, evangelists; and some, pastors and teachers, for the perfecting of the saints, for the work of the ministry, for the edifying of the body of Christ, until we all come in the unity of the faith, and of the knowledge of the Son of God, unto a perfect man, unto the meas-

ure of the stature of the fullness of Christ (Ephesians 4:11-13).

For further study of the Christian way of life, see Bible Studies for a Firm Foundation, by Bob and Rose Weiner. This book can be ordered in paperback from Maranatha Publications, Inc., P. O. Box 1799, Gainesville, FL 32602; phone: 352-375-6000; fax: 352-335-0080. ISBN # 0-938553-005

Appendix B: Classical Books and Authors
on Intercessory Prayer

Basic Intercession 101, by Cindy Jacobs [4 audio tapes], Generals of Intercession, P.O. Box 49788, Colorado Springs, CO 80949-9788

Beyond The Veil, by Alice Smith, Regal Books, Ventura, CA 1-800-4-Gospel

Cross Pollination, by Lila Terhune, Revival Press, Destiny Image, Shippensburg, PA

Destined For The Throne, by Paul E. Billheimer, Bethany House Publishers, 11300 Hampshire Avenue South, Minneapolis, MN 55438

Effective Fervent Prayer, by Mary Alice Isleip, 7476 W. 78th St., Bloomington, MN 55439

Explaining Intercession, by Johannes Facius, Sovereign World Ltd., P. O. Box 777, Tonbridge, Kent TX11 9XT, England

The Fire Of Delayed Answers, by Bob Sorge

How Prayer Brings Revival - Bill Bright, Intercessors For America, PO Box 4477, Leesburg, VA 22075

How To Fast Successfully, by Derek Prince, Intercessors For America, PO Box 4477, Leesburg, VA 22075

Intercession: Thrilling & Fulfilling, by Joy Dawson, YWAM Publishing, Seattle, WA

Intercessory Prayer, by Dutch Sheets, Generals of Intercession, PO Box 49788, Colorado Springs, CO 80949-9788

Making A Prayer Warrior, by Dr. Mildred C. Harris, [audio tape] God First Ministries, P. O. Box 490293, Chicago, IL 60649-0293

Possessing The Gates of The Enemy, by Cindy Jacobs, Generals of Intercession, P.O.Box 49788, Colorado Springs, CO 80949-9788

Power Through Prayer, E. M. Bounds, Zondervan Publishing House, Grand Rapids

The Powerhouse of God, by Johannes Facius, Sovereign World Ltd.

Prayer: Key To Revival, by Paul Y. Cho, Word Publishing, Dallas

The Prayer Life, by Andrew Murray, Whittaker House, Springdale, PA 15144

The Prayer Warrior Series, by C. Peter Wagner [6 books]: 1) Warfare Prayer, 2) Prayer Shield, 3) Breaking Strongholds In Your City, 4) Churches That Pray, 5) Confronting The Powers, 6) Praying With Power, Regal Books, Ventura, CA, 1-800-4-Gospel

Praying Hyde: The Life of John "Praying" Hyde, edited by Captain E. G. Carré

Prophetic Intercession, by Lars Enarson of The Watchman International Inc. [3 audio tapes], P O Box 3670, Pensacola, FL 32516

Purpose In Prayer, E. M. Bounds, Zondervan Publishing House, Grand Rapids, MI

Rees Howells, Intercessor, by Norman Grubb

Restoration: A Direction For Prayer, by Kjell Sjöberg, Intercessors For America

Restoring the Power and Passion of Intercession, Jim W. Goll

The River of God, by Dutch Sheets, Generals of Intercession, Colorado Springs, CO

Seasons of Intercession, by Frank Damazio, BT Publishing, Portland, OR

Seven Basic Steps To Successful Fasting & Prayer, Intercessors For America

Seven Guides To Effective Prayer, by Colin Whittaker, Bethany House Publishers, 11300 Hampshire Avenue South, Minneapolis, MN 55438

Shaping History Through Prayer and Fasting, by Derek Prince, Derek Prince Ministries, P. O. Box 19501, Charlotte, NC 28219-9501

The Voice of God, by Cindy Jacobs, Generals of Intercession, PO Box 49788, Colorado Springs, CO 80949-9788

Winning The Prayer War, by Kjell Sjöberg, Intercessors For America, P.O. Box 4477, Leesburg, VA 22075

Appendix C: Healing Scriptures

Ex. 15:26: And said, If thou wilt diligently hearken to the voice of the LORD thy God, and wilt do that which is right in his sight, and wilt give ear to his commandments, and keep all his statutes, I will put none of these diseases upon thee, which I have brought upon the Egyptians: for I [am] the LORD that healeth thee.

Ex. 23:25: And ye shall serve the LORD your God, and he shall bless thy bread, and thy water; and I will take sickness away from the midst of thee.

Deut. 7:14-15: You will be blessed more than any other people; none of your men or women will be childless, nor any of your livestock without young. 15 The LORD will keep you free from every disease. He will not inflict on you the horrible diseases you knew in Egypt, but he will inflict them on all who hate you.

Deut. 30:19-20: This day I call heaven and earth as witnesses against you that I have set before you life and death, blessings and curses. Now choose life, so that you and your children may live 20 and that you may love the LORD your God, listen to his voice, and hold fast to him. For the LORD is your life, and he will give you many years in the land he swore to give to your fathers, Abraham, Isaac and Jacob.

1 Kgs. 8:56: "Praise be to the LORD, who has given rest to his people Israel just as he promised. Not one word has failed of all the good promises he gave through his servant Moses.

Ps. 91:9-10, 14-16: If you make the Most High your dwelling— even the LORD, who is my refuge— 10 then no harm will befall you, no disaster will come near your tent ... 14 "Because he loves me," says the LORD, "I will rescue him; I will protect him, for he acknowledges my name. 15 He will call upon me, and I will answer him; I will be with him in trouble, I will deliver him and honor him. 16 With long life will I satisfy him and show him my salvation."

Ps. 103:1-5: Praise the LORD, O my soul; all my inmost being, praise his holy name. 2 Bless the LORD, O my soul, and forget not all his benefits— 3 who forgives all your sins and heals all your diseases, 4 who redeems your life from the pit and crowns you with love and compassion, 5 who satisfies your desires with good things so that your youth is renewed like the eagle's.

Ps. 107:19-20: Then they cried to the LORD in their trouble, and he saved them from their distress. 20 He sent forth his word and healed them; he rescued them from the grave.

Ps. 118:17: I will not die but live, and will proclaim what the LORD has done.

Pr. 4:20-24: My son, pay attention to what I say; listen closely to my words. 21 Do not let them out of your sight, keep them within your heart; 22 for they are life to those who find them and health to a man's whole body. 23 Above all else, guard your heart, for it is the wellspring of life. 24 Put away perversity from your mouth; keep corrupt talk far from your lips.

Is. 41:10: So do not fear, for I am with you; do not be dismayed, for I am your God. I will strengthen you and help you; I will uphold you with my righteous right hand.

Is. 53:4-5: Surely he took up our infirmities and carried our sorrows, yet we considered him stricken by God, smitten by him, and afflicted. 5 But he was pierced for our transgressions, he was crushed for our iniquities; the punishment that brought us peace was upon him, and by his wounds we are healed.

Jer. 1:12: The LORD said to me, "You have seen correctly, for I am watching {[12] The Hebrew for watching sounds like the Hebrew for almond tree.} to see that my word is fulfilled."

Jer. 30:17: But I will restore you to health and heal your wounds,' declares the LORD, 'because you are called an outcast, Zion for whom no one cares.'

Joel 3:10: Beat your plowshares into swords and your pruning hooks into spears. Let the weakling say, 'I am strong!'

Nah. 1:9: Whatever they plot against the LORD he {[9] Or What do you foes plot against the LORD? He} will bring to an end; trouble will not come a second time.

Mt. 4:23: Now Jesus went throughout Galilee, teaching in their synagogues, preaching the good news of the kingdom, and healing every disease and sickness among the people.

Mt. 8:2-3: A man with leprosy {[2] The Greek word was used for various diseases affecting the skin—not necessarily leprosy.} came and knelt before him and said, "Lord, if you are willing, you can make me clean." 3 Jesus reached out his hand and touched the man. "I am willing," he said. "Be clean!" Immediately he was cured {[3] Greek made clean} of his leprosy.

Mt. 8:16-17: When evening came, many who were demon-possessed were brought to him, and he drove out the spirits with a word and healed all the sick. 17 This was to fulfill what was spoken through the prophet Isaiah: "He took up our infirmities and carried our diseases." {[17] Isaiah 53:4}

Mt. 18:18-19: "I tell you the truth, whatever you bind on earth will be {[18] Or have been} bound in heaven, and whatever you loose on earth will be {[18] Or have been} loosed in heaven. 19 "Again, I tell you that if two of you on earth agree about anything you ask for, it will be done for you by my Father in heaven.

Mt. 21:21: Jesus replied, "I tell you the truth, if you have faith and do not doubt, not only can you do what was done to the fig tree, but also you can say to this mountain, `Go, throw yourself into the sea,' and it will be done.

Mk. 11:22-24: "Have {[22] Some early manuscripts If you have} faith in God," Jesus answered. 23 "I tell you the truth, if anyone says to this mountain, `Go, throw yourself into the sea,' and does not doubt in his heart but believes that what he says will happen, it will be done for him. 24 Therefore I tell you, whatever you ask for in prayer, believe that you have received it, and it will be yours.

Mk. 16:14-18: Later Jesus appeared to the Eleven as they were eating; he rebuked them for their lack of faith and their stubborn refusal to believe those who had seen him after he had risen. 15 He said to them, "Go into all the world and preach the good news to all creation. 16 Whoever believes and is baptized will be saved, but whoever does not believe will be condemned. 17 And these signs will accompany those who believe: In my name they will drive out demons; they will speak in new tongues; 18 they will pick up snakes with their hands; and when they drink deadly poison, it will not hurt them at all; they will place their hands on sick people, and they will get well."

Rom. 4:16-21: Therefore, the promise comes by faith, so that it may be by grace and may be guaranteed to all Abraham's offspring—not only to those who are of the law but also to those who are of the faith of Abraham. He is the father of us all. 17 As it is written: "I have made you a father of many nations." {[17] Gen. 17:5} He is our father in the sight of God, in whom he believed—the God who gives life to the dead and calls things that are not as though they were. 18 Against all hope, Abraham in hope believed and so became the father of many nations, just as it had been said to him, "So shall your offspring be." {[18] Gen. 15:5} 19 Without weakening in his faith, he faced the fact that his body was as good as dead—since he was about a hundred years old—and that Sarah's womb was also dead. 20 Yet he did not waver through unbelief regarding the promise of God, but was strengthened in his faith and gave glory to God, 21 being fully persuaded that God had power to do what he had promised.

1 Pet. 2:24: He himself bore our sins in his body on the tree, so that we might die to sins and live for righteousness; by his wounds you have been healed.

1 Jn. 3:21-22: Dear friends, if our hearts do not condemn us, we have confidence before God 22 and receive from him anything we ask, because we obey his commands and do what pleases him.

1 Jn. 5:14-15: This is the confidence we have in approaching God: that if we ask anything according to his will, he hears us. 15 And if we know that he hears us—whatever we ask—we know that we have what we asked of him.

3 Jn. 2: Dear friend, I pray that you may enjoy good health and that all may go well with you, even as your soul is getting along well.

Rev. 12:11: They overcame him by the blood of the Lamb and by the word of their testimony; they did not love their lives so much as to shrink from death.

Mal. 4:2: But to you who fear My name the Sun of Righteousness shall arise with healing in His wings...

Jas. 5:15: And the prayer offered in faith will make the sick person well; the Lord will raise him up. If he has sinned, he will be forgiven.

Appendix D: Questions and Answers

This series of diverse questions and answers were given on April 24, 1992, at River of Life Church, Cedar Rapids, Iowa, at the Spring Leadership Conference, entitled "A Time To Seek God" by Pastors Francis Frangipane, Reuven Doron and Marvin Eales. The audience found the answers helpful. The reader may find this session very helpful as an example of a truly spiritual church. Here are the questions from the audience and the answers given:

1) What is the difference between prayer and spiritual warfare? Prayer is an appeal to God for what only God can do. Spiritual warfare is a proclamation to the devil of what God has already done.

2) How do you see the ministry of the River of Life Church? There are three foundational structures or principles for River of Life ministry: An attitude of prayer, humility and Christlikeness. We are more concerned with what we are, than what we do. There are five elders (pastors), a ladies' ministry team and prayer teams. There are about 400 people in the church, which is a symbol of healing, especially healing relationships between churches. Restoration of all things back to Christ is their church goal.

3) What are your favorite books next to the Bible? Francis' favorite author next to the Bible is Andrew Murray, because of his passion for the Lord. Marvin's favorites are Watchman Nees' *Sit, Walk, Stand*, and A. W. Tozier's *Pursuit of God.*

4) Which is the more anointed prayer; when it is easy or

when it is hard to pray? The most anointed prayer is one that has faithfulness and has wisdom. In Acts Cornelius was told: Your prayers and almsgiving have ascended to God. It is not what prayer produces immediately that counts, but what it eventually accomplishes. Look at Anna in the temple; she prayed for many years and was an embarrassment to established religion for no visible results; but fruit eventually was produced. Faithful men and women are what God is looking for! In Mt. 24:45-46 Jesus says: ***"Who then is the faithful and wise servant, whom the master has put in charge of the servants in his household to give them their food at the proper time? It will be good for that servant whose master finds him doing so when he returns."*** With a mixture of humility and faith we have the heart of God; then we have God exactly where **He wants us!** Oh! Hallelujah!

5) How does one gain the gift of discernment? Real discernment comes only when judgment (criticism) stops! Only when our propensity to judge is cleansed from us! The most insidious sin is spiritual pride. He who speaks for himself seeks his own glory (root of pride). He who seeks his own glory will soon judge us and others (as accuser of the brethren). Jesus says in Jn. 5:22: ***"There is one who seeks and judges."***

6) Can one pray against the Jezebel spirit alone? You can deal with the Jezebel spirit when you can deal with Ahab![421] He has to become loving and dismantle the insecurity she uses to protect herself (with false strength). Pray before you ever deal with

---

[421] The Jezebel and Ahab spirits can be found in either men or women; since the Jezebel spirit was first expounded for our instruction in Queen Jezebel and the Ahab Spirit in King Ahab, hence I choose to use the feminie and masculine pronouns of her and his accordingly referring to the Jezebel and Ahab spirit.

this spirit and then there is no need to even mention the Jezebel spirit in removing its influence. Make certain that this spirit is within your sphere of influence or you will not only be ineffective, but you will get slaughtered!

7) What is the woman's role in the church? Men's role is authority and a place of leadership. Women's role is one of delegated authority and leadership depending on the anointing and gifts, such as healing ministry, prophesy or counseling (women are more intuitive).

Dear Reader:

We all have a testimony. If this book witnessed to your life, we would be pleased to hear from you.

Write us a letter that we might be able to use in future publications. Please do not reveal anything in your life that you consider so private that you would not want printed for the public to read. We want you to give glory to God in whatever you write to us.

This will help you crystallize and confirm the testimony of Jesus in your life. "For in him you have been enriched in every way— in all your speaking and in all your knowledge—because our testimony about Christ was confirmed in you." [1 Cor. 1:5,6]

By writing to us we understand that you are giving us permission to publish any portion or all of what you write, if we deem it relevant in some future copyrighted book, magazine or publication.

We are not in a position to give counsel to anyone or even to reply; if you are in need of counsel, please see your pastor.

Also, know that this book can be ordered for some of your friends whom you know would benefit greatly from reading it.

If you desire to be put on our mailing list for any future books, tapes or videos that, God willing, might become available in the future, please check the appropriate box on the next page.

Vern Ihm

———Yes, I am sending you some of my testimony to glorify Jesus.

———Yes, I desire to be put on your mailing list for future works.

———Yes, I am sending you a check [or money order] for my friend[s] to receive ———books, The Testimony of Jesus – Book 1.

Enclosed is $15.00 per copy plus $3.00 for shipping/handling.

My name: _____

Street _____

City _____ State _____ Zip _____

My friend's name: _____

Street _____

City _____ State _____ Zip _____

My friend's name: _____

Street _____

City _____ State _____ Zip _____

Order from:
Laverne C. Ihm
Gold Spirit Ministries, Inc.
2627 N. 114th St.
Milwaukee, WI 53226.

Anyone interested in knowing more, or in helping to support this written word ministry, please contact the scribe by writing to: Gold Spirit Ministries, Inc., 2627 N. 114th Street, Milwaukee, Wisconsin 53226.